PANCHAYATI RAJ FINANCES
IN
MADHYA PRADESH

About the Author

S.K. Singh, Head of the Centre for Panchayati Raj, National Institute for Rural Development (NIRD), Hyderabad, has also worked in the State Finance Commission Division of the Institute. He was associated with an important study on Panchayati Raj Finances, sponsored by the Eleventh Finance Commission, Government of India, covering twenty states of the country. He has to his credit three books and more than sixty research papers.

PANCHAYATI RAJ FINANCES
IN
MADHYA PRADESH

S.K. Singh
Head, Centre for Panchayati Raj
National Institute of Rural Development
Rajendra Nagar, Hyderabad

CONCEPT PUBLISHING COMPANY, NEW DELHI-110059

ISBN 81-8069-062-8

First Published 2004

Published and Printed by
Ashok Kumar Mittal
Concept Publishing Company
A/15-16, Commercial Block, Mohan Garden
NEW DELHI - 110059 (India)

Phones : 25351460, 25351794
Fax : 091-11-25357103
Email : publishing@conceptpub.com

To
My Mother
Smt. Ramkishori Devi
who taught me how to read and write

PREFACE

Decentralised government at the local level as a sequel to the 73rd Constitution Amendment will be key player in national development and local service delivery. To perform these roles they need to be effective and efficient in mobilising and using financial resources. The experiences so far with regard to financial position of panchayats are not encouraging and it is more or less a dependency syndrome. A major concern now is to see how the decentralised system works, particularly in view of disability of mobilising resources.

This study attempts to explore and analyse the existing structure of Panchayati Raj Finances, State-panchayat fiscal relations with special reference to assigned revenues and grants. In the context of Constitutional Amendment, the basic issue is inter-governmental fiscal transfers and flow of funds to panchayats. The devolution of funds mainly depends upon the devolution of functions as envisaged in the provisions of the Constitution under Eleventh Schedule. Besides, flow of funds to panchayats is also on the basis of recommendations of the State Finance Commissions established under the mandated provision of the Constitution. These pertinent issues essentially calls for indepth studies to know the status of financial base of panchayats in the country.

In order to examine critical issues, a study was taken up in the State of Madhya Pradesh to provide the existing financial status of Panchayats and the fiscal relations between the State and Panchayat. To gain deeper insights and practical relevance, the study was conducted in one district, two Janpad Panchayats and four Village Panchayats. Based on primary and secondary sources of data, the study attempts to suggest certain measures as to how to improve the financial situation of Panchayats, particularly mobilisation of internal resources.

In view of the absence of such studies covering various aspects of panchayat finances and critical issues, this study will be of interest to anyone concerned with local finances in decentralised framework. However, it will be of special interest and useful to policy makers, scholars, elected representatives of panchayats, etc.

There are many persons to whom I owe a great deal of gratitude for help and cooperation in this work. At the outset, I express my gratefulness to the National Institute of Rural Development, where presently I am working, to allow me to do this work. I am thankful to the Government of Madhya Pradesh, Department of Panchayats for providing me data and other help in conducting this study. The officers and elected representatives of panchayats in the sample area were kind and cooperative in this task. I express my sincere thanks to my wife Smt. Hemlata Singh for kind cooperation in completing this task. My thanks are also due to my children Sumedha, Suruchi, Samhita and Subedh for their help and full support.

January 2003 S.K. SINGH
Hyderabad

CONTENTS

Preface	vii
List of Tables	xi
List of Graphs	xiii
List of Statements	xiv
1. Introduction	1
2. Functional Devolution on Panchayats	12
3. Financial Composition of Panchayats	28
4. Financial Devolution on Panchayats	68
5. An Overview of State Finance Commission	102
6. Summary and Major Findings	126
Graphs	135
Statements	142
Bibliography	157
Index	159

LIST OF TABLES

3.1	Receipts of Gram Panchayats of Madhya Pradesh	34
3.2	Abstract of Receipts and Expenditure of Gram Panchayats	37
3.3	Composition of Resources of Sample Gram Panchayats	39
3.4	Per Capita Income and Expenditure of Sample Gram Panchayats	41
3.5	Receipts of Janpad Panchayats of Madhya Pradesh	43
3.6	Abstract of Receipts and Expenditure of Janpad Panchayats	45
3.7	Composition of Resources of Sample Janpad Panchayats	47
3.8	Per Capita Income and Expenditure of Sample Janpad Panchayats	49
3.9	Composition of Resources of Zilla Panchayat : Raigarh	52
3.10	Receipts of Zilla Panchayats of Madhya Pradesh	53
3.11	Abstract of Receipts and Expenditure of Zilla Panchayats	55
3.12	Expenditure of Gram Panchayats of Madhya Pradesh	60
3.13	Percentage Expenditure of Gram Panchayats	62
3.14	Expenditure of Janpad Panchayats of Madhya Pradesh	64
3.15	Expenditure of Zilla Panchayats of Madhya Pradesh	66

4.1	Devolution of Assigned Revenues to Zilla Panchayats	75
4A	Criteria for interse Distribution of Funds among Districts Recommended by State Finance Commission	79
4B	Per Capita Assigned Revenue	83
4C	Assigned Revenues from Different Sources Per Capita & Percentage	84
4D	Total Assigned Revenues to Panchayats	85
4E	Total Grants to Panchayats	89
4.2	Devolution of Assigned Revenues to Janpad Panchayats	90
4.3	Devolution of Assigned Revenues to Gram Panchayats	91
4.4	Devolution of Grants to Zilla Panchayats	92
4.5	Devolution of Grants to Janpad Panchayats	93
4.6	Devolution of Grants to Gram Panchayats	94
4.7	Tenth Finance Commission Grant	98
4F	Works to be taken under the Tenth Finance Commission	99

LIST OF GRAPHS

1. Annual Average of Receipts and Expenditure of Sample Gram Panchayats 135
2. Annual Average of Assigned Revenue to Total Receipts of Sample Gram Panchayats 135
3. Annual Average of Assigned Revenue and Grants to Receipts of Sample Gram Panchayats 136
4. Annual Average Assigned Revenue to Expenditure of Sample Gram Panchayats 136
5. Annual Average of Assigned Revenue and Grants to Expenditure of Sample Gram Panchayats 137
6. Annual Average of Own Income to Receipts of Sample Gram Panchayats 137
7. Annual Average of Own Income to Expenditure of Sample Gram Panchayats 138
8. Annual Average of Receipts and Expenditure of Sample Janpad Panchayats 138
9. Annual Average of Assigned Revenue to Receipts of Sample Janpad Panchayats 139
10. Annual Average of Grants to Receipts of Sample Janpad Panchayats 139
11. Annual Average of Assigned Revenue to Expenditure of Sample Janpad Panchayats 140
12. Annual Average of Grants to Expenditure of Sample Janpad Panchayats 140
13. Annual Average of Assigned Revenues and Grants to Receipts of Sample Janpad Panchayats 141
14. Annual Average of Assigned Revenues and Grants to Expenditure of Sample Janpad Panchayats 141

LIST OF STATEMENTS

1.1	Tax and Non-Tax Assigned to Gram Panchayat	142
1.2	Rate of Taxes of Gram Panchayat	144
1.3	Tax and Non-Tax Assigned to Janpad Panchayat	148
1.4	Eleventh Schedule *Vs.* Devolution of Functions to Janpad Panchayat	150
1.5	Eleventh Schedule *Vs.* Devolution of Functions to Zilla Panchayat	152
1.6	Eleventh Schedule *Vs.* Devolution of Functions to Gram Panchayat	154
1.7	Honorarium and other perks to elected representatives	156

1

INTRODUCTION

In a federal set-up, arrangement for inter-governmental financial transfer is essentially a major aspect of public finance. This aspect has become more important when it comes to local government system though they are empowered to raise and utilise financial resources. So far the issues pertaining to mobilisation of finance of the Central and State governments and their existing financial relations are concerned, several studies have been conducted in the past. But, when the question involving the transfer of finance between states and local governments arises, it remained a relatively less explored area particularly in the context of new dispensation of panchayats in the country as a sequel to the 73rd Constitutional Amendment. More so, when the vertical imbalances in terms of resources and expenditure responsibilities are emerging between different layers of government, it calls for transfer of resources from higher level of government to the lower. Keeping the importance and imperatives of fiscal transfers in view, this study has been undertaken to examine critical aspects of State-panchayat fiscal relations in the context of recommendations of the State Finance Commission and response thereupon by the State government.

Federal system of government has several advantages. Among them, it brings economic integration, which promotes industrial and defence capabilities of the country, at the same time the decision-making process is decentralised to suit the politico-economic aspirations of the people at the local level. Through decentralised political and administrative structures, the process of participation of those affected by local decisions is institutionalised and it facilitates better delivery of services to meet local needs and requirements. Moreover, in a decentralised set-up, local governments are more responsive and accountable to people than National/State government. A better linkage between the decision to spend and that to raise resources is established, and thereby fiscal discipline improves. It also allows mobilisation of resources at the local level and hence expected to reduce dependency and strain on Central government. But, in most of the countries of the world, the position of local government finance is almost a dependency situation. Thus, it leads to financial conflicts and persistent demand is made by the local government to higher levels of government to match between financial requirements and functional responsibilities assigned to them. In any federation, as experiences gained so far, a balanced match between finances and functions is a difficult task. Therefore, an indepth analysis of flow of funds to local government is crucial and important, particularly in view of the fiscal imbalances noticed by many countries.

Consequent upon the Amendment of the Indian Constitution (73rd), the number of players in the inter-governmental system increased tremendously, ranging between two to three lakh units of three-tier panchayats in the country. The newly established units will not merely be a set of static institutional arrangements; rather it has to be dynamic and multi-dimensional process that has economic, administrative and political aspects as well. And perhaps, it has risen lot of expectations of the people in rural areas. According to provisions of the Constitution, it has to function as 'institutions of self-government' with the mandatory task of planning for and implementation of economic development and social justice including the items assigned by State Legislatures provided in the Eleventh Schedule (Article 243G). Keeping these aspects in view, the State-panchayat fiscal relations are complex in nature and certainly different than other existing federations in the world.

In the Indian context, the Constitution provides for (Article 243-I & 243-Y) setting up State Finance Commission (SFC) at the state level to review the financial position of the local bodies, both urban and rural, and to make recommendations so as to strengthen the finances of local bodies. While making such recommendations, the Commission will evolve principles which should govern the distribution between the state and the local bodies of the net proceeds of taxes, duties, tolls and fees levied by the state and the determination of taxes, duties, tolls, and fees which may be assigned to or appropriated by the local bodies. The provision also enjoins upon the Commission to lay down the principles, which should govern the grants-in-aid to local bodies from the Consolidated Fund of the State. Besides, Article 280 of the Constitution has been amended by which the National Finance Commission has been mandated to make recommendations regarding the measures needed to augment the Consolidated Funds of States to supplement the resources of local bodies, both rural and urban, on the basis of the recommendations of the State Finance Commission.

Significantly, these Constitutional provisions will have direct bearing upon fiscal federalism in the country as well as the structure of inter-governmental fiscal transfers and relations will pass through vicissitude. Moreover, it intends to rationalise State and sub-State level fiscal relations and make periodic fiscal corrections. The tasks of SFCs are more challenging particularly in the absence of any past experiences, precedence, norms, etc. Therefore, the SFCs have to evolve own normative criteria for devolution of funds to local bodies. Undoubtedly, the establishment of SFC has raised expectations of a large-scale transfer of resources to local bodies from the state kitty. But, the situation is not so, and this expectation raises some pertinent issues—the capacity of States to increase assistance to local bodies and the extent to which the local bodies should depend on them for financial assistance. As the financial situation prevails in most of the states, the scope of financial flow from State to local bodies appears to be quite limited. Thus, it is essential to assess the exact quantum of resource transfer to panchayats as a follow-up to the SFC recommendations.

Rational for Inter-Governmental Transfers

The need for transfer of resources from the State to local government arises because the own revenues of local governments are generally insufficient to meet the expenditure required for providing services allotted to them. Very often, the higher level of government retains the elastic revenue sources; consequently the local government is left with inelastic sources that leads to inadequacy of sources at their disposal. Therefore, a general objective of transfer of resources to local bodies is to supplement their resources so as to enable them to provide services adequately. Moreover, the existing tax bases and tax rates at the disposal of local government are such that it restricts the fiscal capacity. Further, the important factor is that the regional economic imbalances call for purposive transfer of funds on a differential basis.

In the theory of fiscal federalism, the inter-governmental resources transfers are justified on the following grounds:

(i) *Fiscal Gap Correction*: Fiscal gap occurs when there is a mismatch between the expenditure needs and revenue means of the government. Fiscal capacity and fiscal need differ because of several factors. Moreover, the access to revenue base varies from region to region. Also, per unit cost of services varies depending upon geographical conditions and density of population. The fiscal gap may be because of inappropriate assignment of revenue sources and functional responsibilities.

(ii) *Minimum Standard of Services*: Transfer may be required to upgrade the existing level of services to ensure uniform standard across the region.

(iii) *Inter-Jurisdictional Spillovers*: Spillovers (or spatial externalities) occur where the benefits of a locally provided services spread to persons who are not legally required to contribute to the costs of services. The benefits of certain services are generally spillover to neighbouring jurisdictions. Therefore, the inter-governmental grants are the most practical way of correcting for spillover effects.

(iv) *Performance of Agency Functions*: Higher levels of governments may use the services of lower governments to implement certain schemes. Thus, funds are provided for performing such agency functions (Sury, 1998, pp.8-9).

The modern public finance recognises as of fundamental importance the way taxing and spending authorities are delineated and the manner in which inter-governmental transfers are structured in a country. Certain principles have been laid down in designing inter-governmental transfers. Parker (1995) has enunciated the following parameters:

(i) *Transparency* : The basis on which transfers are made, (including any equalisation formula) must be clearly stated;
(ii) *Predictability*: Inter-governmental fiscal transfers mechanism should ensure predictability of sub-national government shares from year to year to permit advanced planning; and
(iii) *Autonomy* : Sub-national governments should have complete independence and flexibility in setting their own development priorities.

Besides these principles, Oommen (1996) has suggested the following criteria for designing the inter-governmental transfers: (a) absorptive capacity — the resource transfer should be in tune with the utilisation capacity, including that of personnel; (b) simplicity — the allocation formula should have adequate built-in-arrangements for encouraging resource mobilisation and penalising waste and uneconomic policies.

Generally, transfers from the higher level to lower level government are made in the form of revenue sharing and grants. In case of panchayats, in the Pre-Amendment period, transfers were mainly in the form of grants. Now, tax sharing has also become another form.

Tax Sharing

The mechanism of tax sharing is quite common in developing countries. A formula based tax sharing is predictable and the recipient government automatically gains from the buoyancy of the shared taxes. Wiseman (1981) argues that it should be based on some criteria. The criteria should have link in the defined specification of responsibility, such as: (i) a scrutiny of locally provided services, with the purpose of distinguishing (a) obligatory local services, (b) discretionary services, (c) activities better administrated by special agency; (ii) a review of local tax and fee sources for identifying local revenues which could be more effective source; (iii) estimating the extent to which the revenue gap should be filled by tax sharing or conditional grants.

There are two types of tax sharing mechanism — the first is called Global Sharing and the second method is Scheduler or Itemised Sharing. In the first method, all tax revenues are pooled for sharing and then certain percentage of the total tax revenue is allocated. In the second method, the sharing of revenue from individual taxes. Tax sharing may take the form of a fixed amount or a fixed proportion of tax revenue.

Grants

Usually, grants are given to reduce horizontal fiscal imbalance to fiscally disadvantaged units. It can also be made conditional regarding its utilisation. Broadly, two types of grants are in vogue. Firstly, General Purpose (or unconditional) Grants, and secondly, Specific Purpose (or conditional) Grants The general purpose grants are given to offset fiscal disadvantages arising from lower taxable capacity or due to higher unit cost of the services provided. It ensures autonomy to use the revenue. The specific purpose grants are usually having conditions attached with it for the achievement of specific objectives. They are used to ensure minimum levels of specified local public services to be provided.

Besides these two types of grants, sometimes grants are provided with matching provisions. This type of grants is called Matching Grants in which it is required that the recipient government should also contribute funds of their own. This has important economic and fiscal advantages in terms of both allocative efficiency and the efficient use of scarce resources.

Another type of grant is Incentive Grants. It is given for the purpose of encouraging the recipient unit to streamline their operations. It depends upon the measures taken by a particular unit to strengthen their financial position.

Evidently, the task of the SFCs is important because they have to rationalise the entire scheme of grants given to local government. The practice of giving grants to local bodies is unsystematic, adhoc, dependency-promoting and of different types (Oommen, 1995). The present study, therefore, seeks to examine the flow of funds to rural local bodies particularly with reference to assigned revenues and grants.

Objectives of the Study

In view of the recent endeavours to strengthen financial base of panchayats, this study has been taken up to provide the present financial status of panchayats and to examine the fiscal relations between the State and Panchayat in the State of Madhya Pradesh. This study has the following broad objectives:

(a) To review State-panchayat fiscal relations in the State; before and after the Action Taken Report (ATR) of the State government on State Finance Commission (SFC) recommendations;

(b) To analyse the criteria and their rationale in the distribution of assigned revenues and grants to Panchayati Raj Institutions (PRIs) in the State before and after ATR of the State government on SFC recommendations;

(c) To assess the executive follow-up and the quantum of resource transfer effected to the PRIs before and after the ATR of the State government on SFC recommendations at the State and field levels; and

(d) To identify the deficiencies and to suggest improvements/ modifications in the existing system and procedures governing distribution of assigned revenues and grants to the PRIs in the State.

Methodology and Study Area

In order to achieve the objectives of the study, various methodological tools were adopted for data collection. Data was collected from primary and secondary sources. A fieldwork was conducted to collect data pertaining to various aspects of the study from different levels. To analyse trends in flow of funds and composition of finances of panchayats at each level, five-year data (wherever available) was collected from the selected units. Besides, to gain deep insights, discussions were held with the concerned officials and elected functionaries of panchayat bodies at each level including officials at the State level. Also, to obtain perception and viewpoints of the people with regard to the finances of panchayats and issues relating to it, discussions were also held with the cross-sections of the society in the sample area. For the purpose, PRA method was used to elicit information. Apart from this, two Gram Sabhas were convened in two village panchayats to have free and frank discussions on the issues pertaining to the study. Also, observation method was used to put things in the right perspective.

This study was conducted in the State of Madhya Pradesh. The selection of the State was due to the fact that

Madhya Pradesh is one of the protagonist states in the country for strengthening the system of panchayats in the post-73rd Constitutional Amendment era. Apparently, the State has gone much ahead with this task and several steps were taken to devolve functions and finances to Panchayati Raj Institutions in the State.

For the purpose of data collection, a district was selected on the basis of average performance, and accordingly, Raigarh district was selected. It is a backward district having predominantly tribal population. Within the selected district, two Janpad Panchayats were selected on the basis of good and average performer in terms of implementation of various programmes. Subsequently, two village panchayats were selected in each Janpad Panchayat, who were good and average performers in terms of developmental programmes. Besides, village panchayats were selected on the backwardness criteria as also to maintain geographic spread of the district. The detail of the study area and its brief profile is given on next page.

Limitations to the Study

This study does suffer from certain limitations on account of various reasons. Time is one of the major constraints. The type of data required in the classified manner was not available and it was difficult to classify for our purposes particularly data pertaining to Gram Panchayats and Janpad Panchayats. Documents were made available in local dialect so it was difficult and took much time to translate them for our use. The record keeping at village level is not proper hence the data supplied to us was not in proper form as also it was not available for five-year period. Hence, in the sample Gram Panchayats, we could not collect five-year data for all selected Gram Panchayats. Similarly, at Zilla Panchayat level, data was not available for five years and the exact receipts and expenditure were not properly maintained.

We also noticed gap in devolution of functions to each layer of panchayat in realistic terms. Data supplied at the

Profile of Study Area

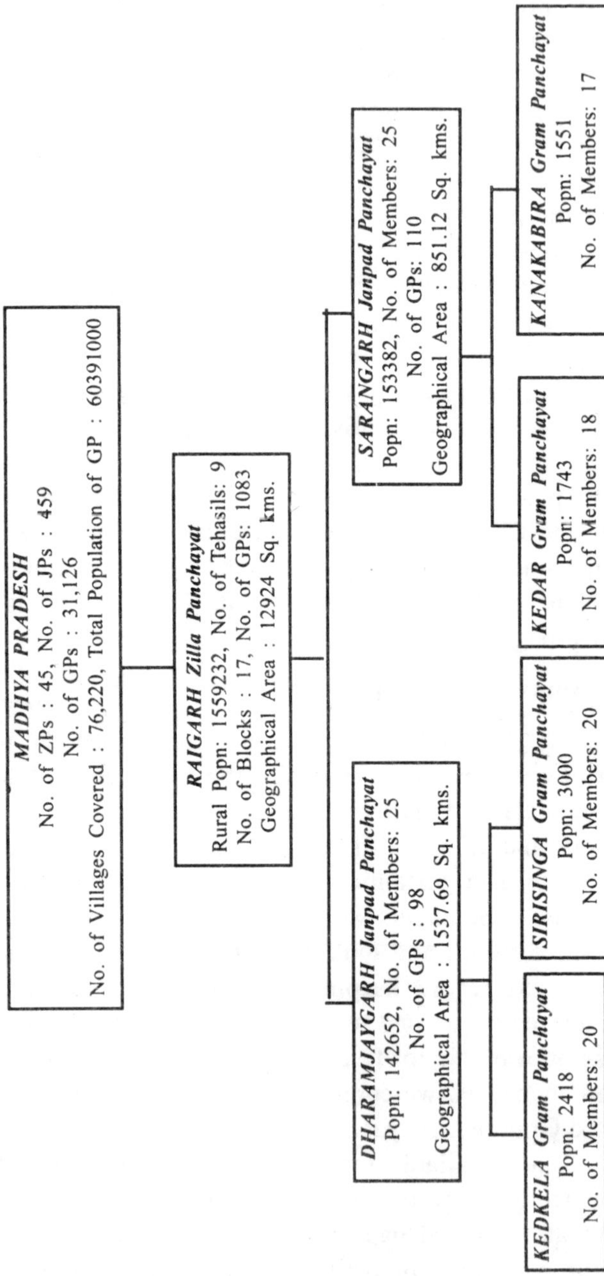

State level also had some confusion. The assigned revenues are given as grants so it was difficult to bifurcate this data into two segments as grants and assigned revenues. Nevertheless, despite several limitations, the report will be useful to get an idea about the panchayat finance and particularly the flow of funds to new set-up of panchayats from higher level of governments in term of grants and assigned revenues, which is the focus of the study. Undoubtedly, we received good cooperation from all concerned during fieldwork.

2

FUNCTIONAL DEVOLUTION ON PANCHAYATS

The financing pattern of panchayats can be examined and decided only in the light of functions assigned to it. Indeed, devolution of funds follows devolution of functions. To determine quantum of funds to flow from the higher levels to lower level of government, expenditure of that unit has to be looked into. Further, to determine the level of expenditure of panchayats, its functional jurisdiction and the standard at which its various functions are performed, these two factors need to be examined. Article 243G envisages devolution of powers to panchayats and it is upto the State Legislature to decide about its functional domain. In view of this, it is necessary to examine what functions, responsibilities and powers are devolved on panchayats in the State in conformity with the provisions of the Constitution.

The Schedule IV of the MPPA, 1993 has reproduced all items listed in the Schedule XI of the Constitution which includes 29 subjects. Though the Constitution under Article 243G has endowed the powers of devolution of functions to panchayats to the State Legislature, but, in turn, the State Legislature has delegated this power to the State government. Section 53(1) of the MP Panchayat Act, 1993 says that the State government by general or special order may entrust to the panchayats preparation of plans and implementation of schemes for economic development and social justice. However, the Act of 1993 does not specify the exact functions relating to these subjects. The State government, in the absence of clear functional devolution in the Act, has issued executive orders in 1994 and 1998 stating the exact activities, responsibilities, programme schemes and projects under 23 departments transferred to three tiers of panchayats (*vide* Chief Secretary's letter of 8th August, 1994). Statements 1.6, 1.4 and 1.5 provide a broad picture of functions transferred to Gram, Janpad and Zilla Panchayats respectively in relation to Schedule XI of the Constitution. However, it is evident from the statements that majority of subjects listed in the Eleventh Schedule has been transferred to them. Further, the executive order delineating functions, followed by circulars issued by various departments indicating functions entrusted to each unit of panchayats, substantiate that steps have been taken in respect of devolution of functions. Nervertheless, these circulars issued by different departments show perfunctory functions entrusted to them like supervision, inspection and selection of beneficiaries.

The functional domain of panchayats can broadly be classified into two — basic functions and agency functions. Basic functions are such core functional activities that are taken up independent of any other agency and these functions are civic and local in nature. Agency functions are such functional responsibilities that are entrusted to any unit to be performed on behalf of other. In this respect, Gram Panchayats have been entrusted with a list of functions of their own, not much relating to agency functions.

Gram Panchayat

Under Section 49 of the Madhya Pradesh Panchayati Raj Adhiniyam, 1993, Gram Panchayats are expected to perform several civic, administrative, regulatory, development and maintenance functions. Some of these functions are as follows:

- Sanitation, construction and maintenance of and cleaning of public streets, latrines, drains, tanks, and other public places. Conversion of step wells, filling of disused wells, etc.

- Lighting of village streets and other public places.
- Construction and maintenance of village roads, culverts, bridges, bunds and other public utility works.
- Regulation of construction and building activities, management of public land.
- Maintenance of Gram Panchayat properties, historical monuments under its care.
- Management of cattle ponds, cattle markets, records relating to cattle.
- Maintenance of records of births and deaths and marriages.
- Promotion of welfare of youth, disabled, destitute and other weaker sections, etc.
- Plantation and preservation of panchayat forests.
- Assistance of Government in Census and other Surveys, in control of diseases, and in preventive measures.
- Other functions entrusted to Gram Panchayats by the Central or State Government or panchayats at the Zilla and Janpad levels.

It can be seen that most of these functions are civic functions, whereas agricultural, social and welfare services are usually undertaken on an agency basis. Among the three tiers of panchayats, only Gram Panchayats have actually been assigned with basic functions like those of urban local bodies. The remaining two levels of panchayats—Janpad and Zilla Panchayats have not been entrusted with any basic functions. They, however, have been entrusted with responsibility of working as an agent of different departments for implementing some of their schemes.

Janpad Panchayat

Janpad Panchayat is entrusted with development, maintenance

and regulatory functions. They have been entrusted with some general administrative functions, such as, provision of emergency relief in calamities, development function and rural development programmes, agriculture and allied activities, control over public health services, public works, development of cottage industries, women and child welfare, welfare of disabled and destitute, etc. In addition, they have some management functions, such as, management of public markets, public melas, etc. They have responsibilities of planning and control over financial as well as human resources. According to Section 51 of the Act, it is obligatory on the part of the Janpad Panchayats to act as agent of government in respect of such functions entrusted by the State government on matters relating to development activities.

Zilla Panchayat

Under the Act of 1993, Zilla Panchayats have been assigned with important functions of planning, co-ordination, allocation of funds to lower level panchayats, recruitment and control of cadres of personnel, development functions, etc. They have not been assigned with any obligatory functions. Evidently, they have to function as agent of the State government.

Assignment of Departmental Activities

Functional responsibilities assigned to panchayats (relating to 23 departments) could be examined in the light of the Chief Secretary's letter dated 8th August 1994 and the circulars issued by different departments (*Paripatron Ka Sankalan* issued on 20th August 1994). It can be seen that involvement of panchayats are mainly in terms of implementation, maintenance, supervision, control, promotion, cooperation, inspection and compliance of Government orders, monitoring and reporting. Generally, functions assigned to the panchayats are as of agents to different departments, whereas only few departments have entrusted the responsibility of implementation of schemes. Gram Panchayats have been made responsible for maintaining the street lights wherever it is available. Panchayats are also responsible for submitting requisitions for extension of road lighting, processing formality for connections for domestic consumers and payment of road lighting monthly bills.

Regarding Village Industries Department, the panchayats have been assigned the responsibility of propagating and making people aware about the various schemes of the departments so that people could take maximum benefits of these programmes. They are also required to make available the list of selected beneficiaries to Village and Khadi Industry Board. The Zilla Panchayats has to establish and manage the training-cum-production centres out of their own resources. But the department has no financial commitment and other assistance for these works.

The panchayats have been assigned the task relating to non-forest areas by the Forest Department. Regarding the availability of funds for performing these functions, it has been mentioned that funds would not be made available for non-forest areas out of the departmental plan budget.

Janpad Panchayats have been assigned with the work relating to the inspection of primary health centres and its overall improvement. For other programmes of the Health Department, they have been entrusted with only the reviewing of programme implementation. They have to supervise the Integrated Child Development Programme and inspect its various centres.

As per the order issued by the Revenue Department, a copy of *patwari* record relating to villages will be given to village panchayats. Village panchayats are responsible for making such records available to villagers for perusal. However, as per the earlier arrangements, the issue of copies and certificates will continue to remain with the Tehsil office.

Water Resources Department has assigned the construction and maintenance of irrigation projects upto 250 hectares to Zilla Panchayats. The administrative approval, budget, inviting tenders for these works will vest with the concerned department executive officers.

Rural Development Department has entrusted the responsibility of implementation and supervision of centrally sponsored scheme Jawahar Rojgar Yojana to panchayats. According to the guidelines, the share of funds allocated to Gram Panchayat under the scheme would be made available to them. Similarly, other centrally sponsored schemes, such as, Indira Awas Yojna, Employment Assurance Scheme, Integrated Rural Development Programme, etc., has been given to panchayats.

Public Health Engineering Department has entrusted maintenance of hand pumps and spot source projects. Initially, for three years the task of maintenance of hand pumps was assigned to Janpad Panchayats and the Zilla Panchayats and they were giving administrative sanction for water supply development works.

The Social Security Pension Yojana of the Social Welfare Department has been entrusted to the panchayats. Applications for pensions will be forwarded and recommended by panchayats after their scrutiny. The Deputy Director of the department will draw the pension amount, and it will be routed through Janpad Panchayats to Gram Panchayats. The Gram Panchayat will distribute the pension amount to the beneficiaries every month in the meeting of village panchayats. Thus, the panchayats are the main implementing agency for the social security pension scheme.

The Animal Husbandry Department has authorised the panchayats to exercise executive control over Veterinary Hospitals and Dispensaries. Fisheries department has authorised the panchayats to lease out tanks falling under their jurisdiction and the revenue collected from it will be deposited in the panchayat.

According to the Department of School Education, all schools of the department would be under the control of Janpad Panchayats. They will be responsible for the establishment of schools as per the allocation within its area. Importantly, they will do the appointment of teachers on prescribed honorarium. For distribution of school uniforms, the Janpad and Zilla Panchayats will accord approval upto Rs. 5 lakhs and Rs. 10 lakhs respectively.

Status of Devolution of Functions

Although panchayats have acquired constitutional status but they are heavily dependent upon the State government for devolution of functions, as mentioned earlier. Evidently, the development works have not been adequately transferred to them. In this regard, the Madhya Pradesh State Finance Commission has also observed that "except a few obligatory functions assigned to rural panchayats under Section 49, the three tier Panchayati Raj Institutions have not been recognised as autonomous units in the strict sense of the terms."*

With regard to the core functions, it was found in the sample Gram Panchayats that they are not fully aware of their powers and responsibilities assigned in the Act, as much as, the circulars issued to give effect to devolution process. Though they were in possession of the circular, even then, they were neither aware of specific works allotted to them nor they were making use of it. In the absence of such knowledge, even regarding the civic services like sanitation, conservancy and abatement of nuisance are not being fully performed by them. Nevertheless, with regard to functions like construction, repair and maintenance of public wells, pond and tanks, the situation in the sample Gram Panchayats were satisfactory to some extent. Surprisingly, majority of the Gram Panchayats mentioned about the mismatch between availability of funds and functions to be performed. Even certain functions, which do not involve finances, are not being effectively carried out. By and large, inability to function effectively is due to dearth of resources and to some extent non-initiative of functionaries. Apparently, the long

* Report for rural local bodies, June, 1996, M.P. State Finance Commission.

list of functions and responsibilities assigned to panchayats has not much practical significance in terms of execution due to obvious reasons. Therefore, execution of civic services need further push in order to meet the expectations and aspirations of people.

Gram Panchayats are implementing various Central and State Schemes of Welfare and alleviation of poverty in rural areas. They are selecting beneficiaries for these schemes. Gram Sabha has to select the beneficiaries. On scanning the minutes of Gram Sabha, it was found that usually it was done in the extended meeting of Gram Sabha in which a few members participate. Therefore, it becomes a show of the Sarpanch than the total involvement of the villagers in the decision-making process. Gram Sabhas are not active and the purpose is not fulfilled for which they have been established.

Janpad Panchayat has been assigned with the function of promotion of organic agriculture and other related aspects of land improvement. It was reported that the Agriculture Department is still carrying out all these functions. Though the administration and maintenance of veterinary dispensaries and animal husbandry services have been entrusted to the Janpad Panchayats, it was reported that they are not directly carrying it out. However, Veterinary Department, on the approval of the Janpad Panchayat, carry out works relating to breed improvement of livestock, poultry and control of contagious diseases. Granting of lease for pisciculture in tanks, with an average water spread ranging from 10-100 hectares; appointment of Anganwadi workers and assistants; supervision of activities of Primary Health Centres and Subsidiary Health Centres, and encouragement to social forestry is being undertaken by them.

The Education Department on the administrative approval of the Janpad Panchayats is carrying out the construction, extension and maintenance of primary school buildings. However, they do the recruitment of teachers. In a frank disclosure, the functionaries of Janpad Panchayat reported that it becomes difficult to sustain the external influences brought on them in the recruitment of teachers. Janpad Panchayat does the distribution of uniforms to girl students. Thus, Janpad Panchayats are, to some extent, performing assigned tasks.

Zilla Panchayats are preparing development plans, integrating plans prepared by Janpad Panchayats within the district and, in turn, forwarding the integrated plan of the district to the State government. The Zilla Panchayat is carrying out schemes of poverty alleviation and social justice. The DRDA has since been merged with the Zilla Panchayat, they are supervising and fixing targets for the poverty alleviation programme. Zilla Panchayat accords administrative sanction for the works upto Rs. 10 lakhs. Despite the merger of DRDA with Zilla Panchayat, a clear functional division could be seen among the erstwhile staff of Zilla Panchyat and DRDA. The process of functional assimilation and interchange of works among them may take some more time.

Staffing Pattern

Earlier, a Village Assistant was posted at Gram Panchayats to function as its Secretary. In some cases, a Village Assistant was responsible for looking after the works of more than one Gram Panchayat. In the new dispensation, the Government decided to provide Panchayat Secretary in every Gram Panchayat (*vide* Chief Secretary's letter No. 356/C.S./P/94 dated 8th August 1994). Earlier, only 8800 Village Assistants were in position. To manage 31126 Gram Panchayats in the new set-up, they have been authorised, according to the circular, to make alternative arrangement by entrusting the additional charge of Panchayat Secretary to Instructors appointed under non-formal education by paying them monthly honorarium of Rs.200. Subsequently, another notification was issued (*vide* Order No. F-2/12/22/P-1/95 dated 12.9.1995) by the State Government to appoint 'Panchayat Karmi' on a monthly honorarium of Rs. 500 (now raised to Rs.1000) to function as Secretary in Gram Panchayats where Village

Assistants are not yet posted as per earlier order. The above order also declared the post of Village Assistant as 'dying cadre', and no fresh appointment of Village Assistant will be made in future. As per the September 1995 notification, the Panchayat Karmi will be completely under the administrative control of the concerned Gram Panchayat. Further, in partial modification of the above order (*vide* Order No. F-2-12/22/P-1/95, dated 30th October 1996), it was declared that the Panchayat Karmi will be administratively accountable to the CEO of Janpad Panchayat.

As per the Chief Secretary's order dated 8th August 1994, the Chief Executive Officer (CEO) in Janpad Panchayats will be posted from among the junior scale officer of the State Civil Services or from class II grade officers of the Development Departments. Earlier, the prescribed staff structure for each Janpad Panchayat was: Head Clerk (1), LDC (4), Steno typist (1), Peon (2) and *Chaukidar* (1). The staff strength continued to be the same till the merger of Block Development Office in Janpad Panchayats in October, 1997 (*vide* Panchayat and Rural Development Department Order No. 3-7/95/22/8-2 dated 13th October, 1995). Now the Block Development Officer posted in the Development Block has been designated as Additional Chief Executive Officers in the respective Janpad Panchayat (*vide* Panchayat and Rural Development order No. 1-2-3/22/P-1/95 dated 6th January, 1995). Further, another order was issued (*vide* Order No. 3f/30/97/22/P-1 dated 6th December, 1997) restricting the Janpad Panchayats for creating additional posts of Assistant Accounts Officers and part-time sweepers.

Earlier for Zilla Panchayats, it was decided by the State government to post the District Collector as Chief Executive Officer (CEO). And, to assist him in the routine works of the Zilla Panchayat, an officer either from the Indian Administrative Services or from other Development Department will be posted as Additional CEO (*vide* Notification No.1125/1840/22/P-2/94 dated 22nd July 1994). The staffing pattern sanctioned for each Zilla Panchayat before the 73rd Amendment was one post each of Head Clerk/Accountant, Assistant Grade-II, Assistant Grade-III, Driver, *Chaukidar* and Sweeper and two posts of Peon. This staff strength continued till the merger of DRDA in Zilla Panchayat in October 1997 (*vide* Order No. 3-7/95/22/8-2 dated 13th October 1995). Further in 1997, the Zilla Panchayats were restructured by creation of a few new post (*vide* Order No. 3/30/97/22/P-1 dated 6th December 1997). The new restructuring pattern is not uniform pattern for all the Zilla Panchayats. Some posts are common for all districts, while a few posts are based on the size of the district depending upon the number of development blocks. To illustrate, the post of Assistant Accounts Officer has been provided in 24 districts that have more than eight development blocks and less than sixteen development blocks. In five big districts, where development blocks are more than sixteen, one post of Chief Accounts Officer has been provided. The staffs of grade Class III and Class IV of Development Branch of the Collectorate and Director of Panchayat and Social Welfare have been merged (*vide* the order dated 6th December 1997). This has been declared as dying cadre and, therefore, these departments will not recruit any person in future. Surplus staff of government departments will be absorbed against the additional posts created in the panchayats.

Initially, as mentioned above, the Collector was made *exofficio* Chief Executive Officer of Zilla Panchayat who was assisted by a full-time Additional Chief Executive Officer. This scheme was replicated from the West Bengal experience but it did not succeed in the State for the obvious reasons. As revealed, the Collectors were not mentally prepared to work under any elected representative at the district level. Consequently, the Government decided to post a full time CEO. Presently, the CEO is drawn from Indian Administrative Service who is also the Executive Director of DRDA.

In the study area, similar staffing pattern was available. At the Zilla Panchayat level, it was reported that there is a discrimination between the original staff of Zilla Panchayat and DRDA staff in terms of service condition and pay structure. The erstwhile Zilla Panchayat staff is demanding to make their service conditions at par with the DRDA staff. Functionally, DRDA staff does not take up works relating to Zilla Panchayat despite its merger, and they exclusively work for DRDA. Therefore, there is an urgent need to shuffle functional responsibilities among two sets of staff. At the Janpad level, similar differences were found among the erstwhile Janpad staff and Block Development Office staff in terms of service conditions and functional responsibilities despite merger of the two sets of units.

In fine, the functional devolution on panchayats has not been completely operationalised despite various notifications of the government. Therefore, a serious effort should be made to operationalise these notifications *in toto*. Moreover, panchayat functionaries should be sensitised with regard to their responsibilities as per these devolution efforts.

The organisational set-up of three-tier panchayats in the State is given (on pages 24 to 27) along with the staff positions. This will give brief idea about the existing administrative apparatus at each level. So far the Standing Committees are concerned, they have been constituted, but its functional aspect is not very effective. Regarding the staff position, government has prescribed norms for a staff pattern of each unit, but all staff is not deployed at each level.

Organisational Structure of Gram Panchayat

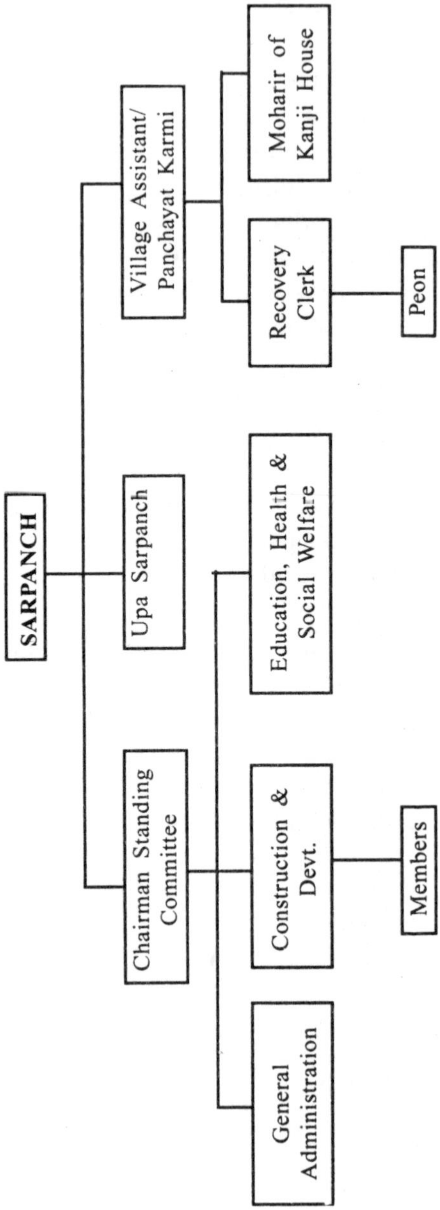

Organizational Structure of Janpad Panchayats

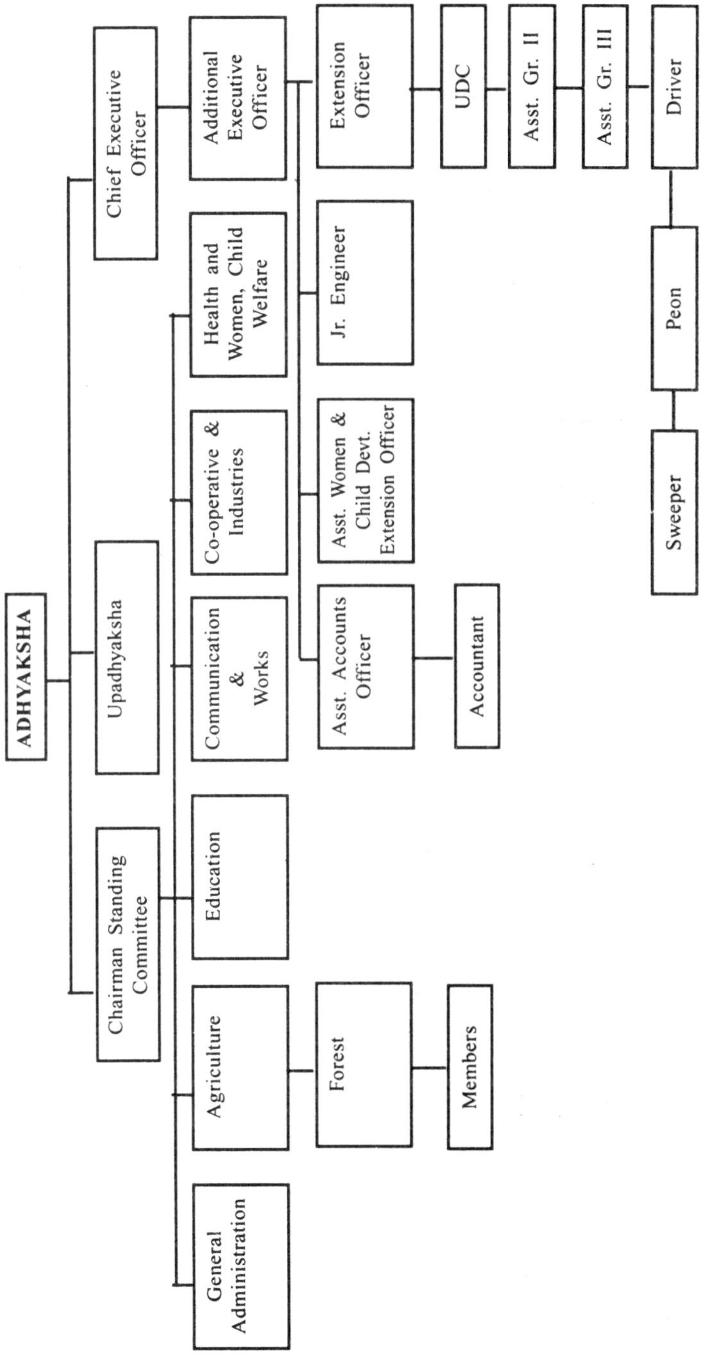

Organizational Structure of Zilla Panchayat

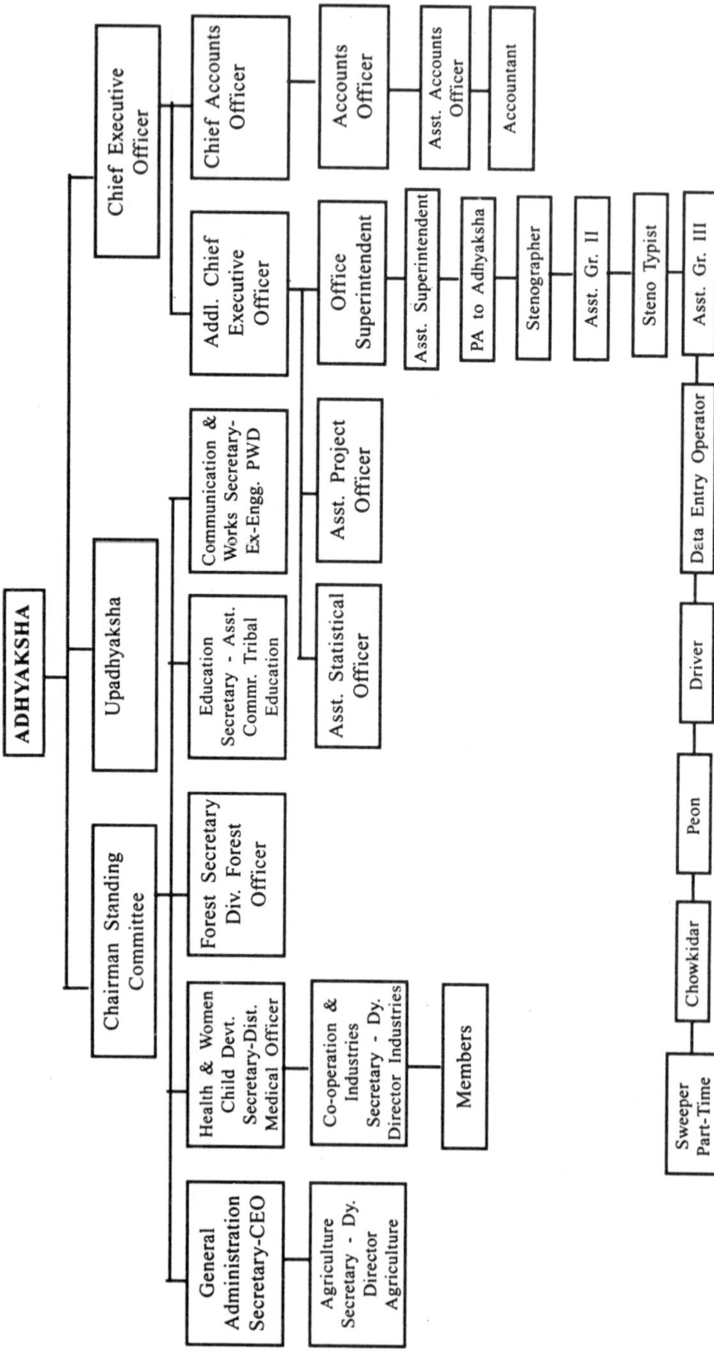

TOTAL STRENGTH OF STAFF (1998-99)

Gram Panchayat

Designation	Staff Sanctioned	Staff in Position
Village Assistant	10177	7603
Recovery clerk	920	918
Moharir of Kanji House	7193	6000
Panchayat Karmi	22954	22954

Janpad Panchayat

Designation	Staff Sanctioned	Staff in Position
Chief Executive Officer	459	—
Addl. CEO	459	—
Asst. Accounts Officer	459	—
UDC/Accountant	459	—
Asst. Grade-II	459	—
Asst. Grade-III	1836	—
Peon	918	—
Sweeper/Farash	5508	—

Zilla Panchayat

Designation	Staff Sanctioned	Staff in Position
Chief Executive Officer	61	61
Additional Chief Executive Officer	122	122
Chief Accounts Officer	61	61
Accounts Officer	61	61
Asst. Accounts Officer	61	61
APO	236	236
Office Supdt.	61	61
ASO	61	61
Asst. Supdt.	122	122
Accountant	189	189
AIPR	61	61
PA to Chairman	61	61
Stenographer	122	122
Asst. Grade-II	488	488
Steno Typist	188	188
Data Entry Operator	81	81
Asst. Grade-III	652	652
Driver	129	129
Peon	283	283
Chowkidar	61	61
Farash/Sweeper (Part time)	61	61

3

FINANCIAL COMPOSITION OF PANCHAYATS

In order to examine State-Panchayat Fiscal relations, it is essential to review the financial composition of panchayats. Notwithstanding the fact that panchayats are suffering from inadequacy of resources but also they are not in a position to generate sufficient income to reach to the level of self-sufficiency. Generally, the finances of panchayats are from three major sources: (i) own resources, which include tax and non-tax revenue, (ii) assigned revenues, and (iii) grants-in-aid. In this chapter we will examine only one source of revenues, that is, from own sources as the other sources of revenue has been discussed in the next chapter. We will also examine the expenditure of panchayats to have an overview of the financial composition of panchayats. In own resource, two important components are included; they are tax and non-tax revenues. Besides, we will also examine the overall trends and patterns of expenditure of panchayats so as to ascertain their fiscal needs in light of functional devolution.

Tax-Revenues

The revenue raising power is important in view of self-sufficiency and fiscal autonomy. Generally, panchayats at each level are assigned number of taxes but majority of them are not buoyant and elastic source. Besides, panchayats have several problems in tax administration. The MP Panchayat Adhiniyam, 1993 empowers panchayats to levy and collect several taxes. There is no difference between the earlier

Panchayat Acts of 1981 and 1990 with the existing Act of 1993 as far as the taxation powers are concerned. In other words, taxes assigned to panchayats in the Pre- and Post-73rd Amendment period has not changed. By and large, the principles or consideration for taxation powers also remained the same.

Gram Panchayat

In the Act of 1993, Section 77 (alongwith the Schedule I, II & III) provides taxation powers of Gram Panchayat and Janpad Panchayat. These bodies are empowered with two types of taxation powers — (i) obligatory taxes, and (ii) optional taxes and fees. Statement 1.1 provides the list of taxes that Gram Panchayat can levy, it also includes both categories of tax items. Among the important obligatory taxes, Gram Panchayats are empowered to levy property tax, lighting tax and profession tax. In the optional tax items, important is vehicle tax and water tax. They are also empowered to levy other tax items for which the State Legislature is empowered under the Constitution. It is clear from the list that Gram Panchayats are vested with such taxation powers and items, which are usually given to these bodies. Though it contains a long list, only few items are in operation. And even some of the compulsory taxes are not being levied due to various reasons. Moreover, some of the tax items do not have much scope and potential to raise revenue, if imposed even. The services rendered by panchayats are usually unsatisfactory hence people are not willing to pay taxes. More so, the available infrastructure is inadequate to the extent that better delivery of services cannot be provided.

Rates of each tax item of Gram Panchayat prevailing before and after the 73rd Amendment is given in Statement 1.2. It can be seen that the existing rates have been enhanced from the earlier rates for all items. Thus, the scope for raising revenue has been enlarged. As the government is empowered to prescribe rates of taxable items, a pertinent issue needs consideration whether these units should be allowed to fix rates themselves or the government should prescribe minimum and maximum rates. The rates are since prescribed for all items; therefore, the autonomy of panchayats to fix rates is taken away. Among the taxes, the rates of profession tax have remarkably increased which could augment more revenues. But, in fact, very few units levy this tax and revenue mobilisation is not to the expectation.

Janpad Panchayat

Janpad Panchayat has only one compulsory tax under their domain, that is, entertainment tax. Among the optional taxes, Janpad Panchayat can levy development tax on agriculture land and additional stamp duty. The rates of entertainment tax have been prescribed under rules notified by the government. It can be seen in the Statement 1.3 that the existing rates have been doubled than the earlier, even then, it is quite low as compared to other states. This revision has taken place after thirty years. In case of development tax on agriculture land, it is rarely utilised by them although it could be a good source of income in view of modernisation taking place in the agriculture sector.

Zilla Panchayat

Zilla Panchayat in the State is not vested with any taxation power. According to the amendment of 1997 in the present Panchayat Act of 1993, Zilla Panchayat has been empowered to increase the rate of cess on land revenue to the extent of Rs.10 on every rupee of land revenue. This additional cess income will be distributed among Zilla Panchayat, Janpad Panchayat and Gram Panchayat in the ratio of 25:25:50 respectively. Surprisingly, no Zilla Panchayat has exercised this power so far and hence no income is generated.

Procedure for Levying Tax or Fee

The following procedure is to be maintained before imposing tax by Gram Panchayat:

(i) A resolution has to be passed for the rate at which the tax or fee is to be imposed.
(ii) The rates so fixed have to be notified to the public by drumbeats or affixing notice at conspicuous place.
(iii) After considering objections/suggestions, rates finally decided will have to be again notified.

As seen above, the taxation power of these bodies have not changed for a long time. Despite the revision of rates prescribed with minimum and maximum, the tax net has not increased, and it absolute terms it is not giving higher revenue. The reasons are that the size of Gram Panchayats are small (average population 1736), for Janpad Panchayats the population size varies from 34972 to 293668. Secondly, about 43 per cent people in rural area are below poverty line hence a large portion of rural population is out of the tax net. Thirdly, the tax administration is not up to mark. Fourthly, initiative of local leaders, particularly of reserve categories, to raise revenue is discouraging and their perception in this matter is awful.

Non-Tax Revenues

Gram Panchayat

The non-tax sources of revenues for Gram Panchayat are given in Statement 1.1. In this sphere, Gram Panchayats have been assigned two types of sources, that is, obligatory and optional sources. In the obligatory non-tax sources, Gram Panchayats are empowered to levy market fees and fees on registration of cattle. Among the optional category, a good number of items have been listed for levying. These items have not changed from the old Act and continue to be the same.

The comparative rates of non-tax sources that are prevailing before and after the amendment, as seen in the Statement 1.2, have undergone changes and increased. The new rates have been modified as per the notification of the government on 29th February, 1996. Under the provisions of the Act of 1993, a Gram Panchayat is required to place the proposal for imposing any tax/fee in the meeting of Gram Sabha. After resolving to impose any tax or fee, it shall have to proclaim the resolution for information of the public by beat of drum or written notice affixed at Gram Panchayat office or any conspicuous place in the area or both. After considering the objections, if any, and getting the clearance from the Janpad Panchayat, the Gram Panchayat adopts the taxes/fees to be imposed. It is required that the schedules of rates fixed are to be notified in usual procedure as stated earlier. The Janpad Panchayat while approving the proposal specifies the date from which the tax or fee mentioned therein should come into force.

Janpad Panchayat

In the non-tax sources of revenue, Janpad Panchayats are empowered to levy fees for any licence for use and occupation of land or other property (see Statement 1.3). In addition to this, they are empowered to auction/lease ferry services and impose fines on defaulters of payment of tax. A comparative prescribed rates is given in the Statement 1.3. The powers are the same as compared to earlier powers and changes in rates has been notified. Regarding ferry services, they are empowered to auction it.

Zilla Panchayat

Among non-tax sources, Zilla Panchayats have been vested

with power to raise resources from water bodies (tanks) within their jurisdiction. Statement 1.3 provides the classification according to the size of water bodies for which each tier is vested with powers. Generally, Zilla Panchayat sources of revenue from non-tax are fishery rental (leasing of tanks), rent or fee from property. Therefore, Zilla Panchayat has limited sources of non-tax revenue.

Trends in Local Revenue Mobilisation

After discussing about the tax and non-tax sources and their prevailing rates in the State, we will now examine the trends in local resource mobilisation by these bodies. In fact, lots of variations exist across the states in the overall magnitude of resources mobilised by panchayats from taxes and non-tax sources. The wide variation in magnitude of incomes of panchayats from one State to another and even among the panchayats within one State is due to size of panchayats in terms of population coverage. Discussions presented below will broadly give an idea about the trends in the internal resources mobilisation by these bodies.

Tax Revenues

Table 3.1 provides six years data of total receipts from all sources itemwise for all Gram Panchayats in the State. Evidently, the per capita income from any taxable item is either slightly higher than one rupee or less than one rupee. Increase in per capita income from property tax, profession tax, water rate and lighting rate is noticed over a period of time, but it is not much significant. Other two taxable items (Drainage tax and Building rent) does not show increase, rather it is fluctuating. It is expected that property tax and profession tax could have given more income to panchayats, as these items have scope and potential, but it is not. Among the taxes, contribution of water tax is the highest and more than other sources and it is showing steady increase. Even,

Table 3.1 : Receipts of Gram Panchayats of Madhya Pradesh

S.No	Items	1992-93		1993-94		1994-95		1995-96		1996-97		1997-98	
		Amount	PC	Amount	PC	Amount	PC	Amount	PC	Amount	PC	Amount	PC
(1)	(2)	(3)	(4)	(5)	(6)	(7)	(8)	(9)	(10)	(11)	(12)	(13)	(14)
A.	**Tax Revenue**												
(i)	Property	11156	0.32	14368	0.41	26325	0.75	19125	0.55	26008	0.76	26528	0.76
(ii)	Profession	2173	0.06	890	0.03	2037	0.06	2547	0.07	2255	0.06	2300	0.07
(iii)	Water Rate	15901	0.46	25072	0.72	35082	1.01	46068	1.32	45828	1.31	46745	1.34
(iv)	Lighting Rate	6375	0.18	6492	0.19	12283	0.35	12202	0.35	13556	0.39	13827	0.40
(v)	Drainage Tax	436	0.01	72	0.00	89	0.00	95	0.00	336	0.01	343	0.01
(vi)	Building Rent	9528	0.27	5648	0.16	8028	0.23	9814	0.28	10255	0.29	10460	0.30
	Total Tax Revenue	45569	1.30	52542	1.51	83844	2.40	89851	2.57	98238	2.82	100203	2.88
B.	**Non-Tax Revenue**												
(i)	Fairs, Market and Festivals	14350	0.41	17651	0.51	33582	0.96	28816	0.83	24387	0.70	24875	0.71
(ii)	Fishery Rental	3286	0.09	6135	0.18	9480	0.27	9319	0.27	18591	0.53	18963	0.54
(iii)	Bus Stand Fees	729	0.02	318	0.01	770	0.02	652	0.02	1200	0.03	1224	0.04
(iv)	Cart Stand	155	0.00	195	0.01	315	0.01	387	0.01	341	0.01	348	0.01
(v)	Ferry Service	17585	0.50	18563	0.53	35456	1.02	33807	0.97	35822	1.03	36538	1.05
(vi)	Fines and Penalties	51	0.00	40	0.00	879	0.03	794	0.02	806	0.02	822	0.02
(vii)	Fees for ZP Shelters (Kanji House)	14396	0.41	15046	0.43	21055	0.60	23593	0.68	23902	0.69	24380	0.70
(viii)	Any Other Fees (Market & Other)	45138	1.29	31017	0.89	42645	1.22	53785	1.54	54211	1.55	55295	1.59
(ix)	Animal Registration Fee	2617	0.08	2435	0.07	4051	0.12	5180	0.15	6586	0.19	6718	0.19
(x)	Interest	2170	0.06	2097	0.06	2255	0.06	2458	0.07	2458	0.07	2458	0.07
	Total Non-Tax Revenue	100477	2.86	93497	2.69	150488	4.31	158791	4.56	168304	4.82	171621	4.92
	Total Local Revenue (A+B)	146046	4.16	146039	4.2	234332	6.71	248642	7.13	266542	7.64	271824	7.8

Table 3.1 *(Contd.)*

(1)	(2)	(3)	(4)	(5)	(6)	(7)	(8)	(9)	(10)	(11)	(12)	(13)	(14)
C.	**Assigned Revenues**												
(i)	Surcharge on Commercial Tax												
(ii)	Local Cess	2280	0.07	2280	0.07	2280	0.07	2280	0.07	2280	0.07	3800	0.11
(iii)	Mines and Minerals									4141	0.12	4224	0.12
(iv)	Land Revenue	22500	0.65	22500	0.65	22500	0.65	22500	0.65	22500	0.65	75000	2.15
	Total Assigned Revenues	24780	0.72	24780	0.72	24780	0.72	24780	0.72	28921	0.84	83024	2.38
D.	**Grants-in-Aid (State)**												
(i)	General Purpose Grant from State Govt.	292422	8.39	382877	10.98	377008	10.81	527039	15.11	720484	20.66	742377	21.29
(ii)	Specific Purpose Grant (Basic F. of G.P.)											1673050	47.98
(iii)	Grant for Development Purpose												
E.	**TFC Grants**									771700	22.13	771700	22.13
(i)	Centrally spons.Sch.State	569531	16.33	490070	14.05	488021	14.00	655758	18.81	313238	8.98	619758	17.77
(ii)	Centrally spons.Sch.Central	2007170	57.56	1960279	56.22	1675978	48.06	2554949	73.27	2347416	67.32	2662534	76.36
	Sub-Total (D+E)	2869123	82.28	2833226	81.25	2541007	72.87	3737746	107.19	4152838	119.09	6469419	185.53
GRAND TOTAL		3039949	87.16	3004045	86.17	2800119	80.3	4011168	115.04	4448301	127.57	6824267	195.71

AMOUNT (Rs. Thousands) PC = PER CAPITA (Rupees)

Source: Commissioner of Panchayats, Government of Madhya Pradesh.

the per capita income from all taxable items put together, is not significant and it ranges between Rupees 1.30 to Rupees 2.88. Nevertheless, it is showing increasing trend steadily and it has become more than double in six years.

Table 3.2 shows that the percentage of tax revenue to the total receipt for Gram Panchayat is minimum 1.5 per cent in 1992-93 and maximum 2.99 per cent in 1994-95. Thus, the contribution of tax revenue is not much significant and obviously Gram Panchayats are depending much on other sources. The percentage increase in tax revenue has gone up maximum to 59 per cent in 1994-95 and minimum to 7 per cent in 1995-96. Nevertheless, it is always increasing and it has become more than double in absolute terms in five year period. Such wide variation reflects on the mechanism of tax collection and it may be due to the collection of more arrears in a particular year and increase in rates. Also, the sharp variation in the increase justifies the scope and potential of available tax sources, if the tax administration improves.

In its report, the State Finance Commission (1996), based on data collected from sample Gram Panchayats, observed that only 36 per cent of sample Gram Panchayats have imposed property tax, 26 per cent have imposed lighting tax and utilisation of sanitation tax is negligible as it is 3 per cent only. The Commission further observed that hardly about one-third Gram Panchayats collect property tax, however, after the 73rd Amendment there has been some increase in the imposition of property tax. In case of lighting tax, though about 93 per cent villages are reported to be electrified and about 34 per cent households have access to electricity but realisation is not to that extent. The imposition of sanitation tax is about 3 per cent which is quite obvious in view of the number of households (about 4 per cent) having toilet facilities in rural areas of the State. More so, in case of profession tax, there was an increase in utilising this tax after the 73rd Amendment as compared to earlier, but thereafter in 1994-95 it shows declining trend. There could be possibility

Table 3.2 : Abstract of Receipts and Expenditure of Gram Panchayats

S.No	Items	1992-93	1993-94	% of increase	1994-95	% of increase	1995-96	% of increase	1996-97	% of increase	1997-98
1.	Tax Revenue	45569	52542	15.3	83844	59.6	89851	7.2	98238	9.3	100203
	% of Total	1.50	1.75		2.99		2.24		2.21		1.47
2.	Non-Tax Revenue	100477	93497	-6.9	150488	61.0	158791	5.5	168304	6.0	171621
	% of Total	3.31	3.11		5.37		3.96		3.78		2.51
3.	Assigned Revenue	24780	24780	0.0	24780	0.0	24780	0.0	28921	16.7	83024
	% of Total	0.82	0.82		0.88		0.62		0.65		1.22
4.	Grant-in-Aid	292422	382877	30.93	377008	-1.53	527039	39.80	720484	36.7	2415427
	% of Total	9.62	12.75		13.46		13.14		16.20		35.39
5.	TFC & Centrally Sponsored Schemes	2576701	2450349	-4.90	2163999	-11.69	3210707	48.37	3432354	6.90	4053992
	% of Total	84.76	81.57		77.28		80.04		77.16		59.41
	Total Receipt	3039949	3004045	34.38	2800119	107.31	4011168	100.85	4448301	75.64	6824267
	Total Expenditure	3098807	3061131	-1.22	2842724	-7.13	4141523	45.69	4660366	12.53	7076786

Source : Commissioner of Panchayats, Government of Madhya Pradesh.

of decline due to increase in the minimum annual income level from Rs.500 to Rs.11,000 in 1996; the number of persons coming into the tax net would have decreased. But even then, the coverage is not to the full extent. The less coverage of profession tax in rural areas can be substantiated by the explanation given by the sample Gram Panchayats of this study that they are quite hesitant in exercising this power. Regarding realisation of water tax, the Commission further found that since it is to be collected only if portable water is supplied through water supply system, so it has limitations. Moreover, due to non-functional water supply systems in many cases, Gram Panchayats may not have wide coverage. Hence revenue raising from this source has limitations.

Gram Panchayat

Table 3.1 provides composition of resources of sample Gram Panchayat covered under this study. Out of four sample Gram Panchayats, one Gram Panchayat (Kedar) does not have any income from tax revenue since it has predominantly tribal population. The annual average of income from tax sources ranges between Rupees 15 thousand (Kedkela) to nil (Kedar), two others have less than one thousand. This shows that performance of tax revenue fluctuates sharply. The column 14 of Table 3.3 provides the percentage of tax revenue to the total internal resources including non-tax revenue. It can be seen that one Gram Panchayat (Kedkela) has sizeable income from tax revenue to the total internal resources (maximum 75 per cent) and it shows increasing trend and the annual average income from tax revenue comes to 49 per cent which is encouraging. But, in case of other sample Gram Panchayats, it is only 5 to 6 per cent. The per capita income from tax revenue in the sample GPs (Table 3.4) varies from minimum of 3 paisa to maximum of Rs. 7.94 (Kedkela, 1997-98). It can, therefore, be said that there is a scope for mobilising resources through tax income. It depends more on local leadership to take initiative to raise revenue from

Table 3.3 : Composition of Resources of Sample Gram Panchayats

Year	Internal Tax	Resource Non-Tax	Total (2+3)	Assigned Revenues	JRY	Grant-in-Aid others	Total (6+7)	Total (5+8)	Grand Total of Receipts
(1)	(2)	(3)	(4)	(5)	(6)	(7)	(8)	(9)	(10)
1. Kedkela (Population : 2418)									
1996-97	3731	15435	19166	2179	96287	86240	182527	184706	203872
1997-98	19205	17381	36586	0	112360	147957	260317	260317	296903
1998-99	23435	7501	30936	3193	33253	164953	198206	201399	232335
(upto 11/98)									
Annual Average	15457	13439	28896	1790.67	80633.33	133050	213683.3	215474	244370
2. Sisringa (Population : 3000)									
1994-95	104	6628	6732	0	100734	18030	118764	118764	125496
1995-96	2411	9700	12111	1430	97692	30601	128293	129723	141834
1996-97	510	15457	15967	2641	97935	91100	189035	191676	207643
1997-98	0	6980	6980	1074	99000	145400	244400	245474	252454
Annual Average	756.25	9691.25	10447.5	1286.25	98840.25	71282.75	170123	171409.3	181856.75
3. Kedar (Population: 1743)									
1995-96	0	23382	23382	816	14025	127219	141244	142060	165442
1996-97	0	23390	23390	1526	30085	243819	273904	275430	298820
1997-98	0	28191	28191	1047	29115	129346	158461	159508	187699
Annual Average	0	24987.67	24987.7	1129.67	4408.33	166794.67	191203	192332.7	217320.33
4. Kanakbira (Population : 1551)									
1995-96	300	14312	14612	2171	39788	35815	75603	77774	92386
1996-97	2040	14550	16590	1403	44274	78982	123256	124659	141249
1997-98	575	15772	16347	1351	44111	410725	454836	456187	472534
Annual Average	971.67	14878	15849.7	1641.67	42724.33	175174	217898.3	219540	235389.67

Source : Respective Village Panchayats.

Table 3.3 (*Contd.*)

Year	Total Expen-diture	Col. 4 as % of Col. 10	Col. 4 as % of Col. 11	Col. 2 as % of Col.4	Col 5 as % of Col.10	Col. 9 as % of Col.10	Col. 5 as % of Col.11	Col. 9 as % of Col.11
(1)	(11)	(12)	(13)	(14)	(15)	(16)	(17)	(18)
1. Kedkela (Population : 2418)								
1996-97	206839	9.4	9.27	19.47	1.07	90.6	1.05	89.3
1997-98	278943	12.32	13.13	52.49	0	87.68	0	93.32
1998-99 (upto 11/98)	233254	13.32	13.26	75.75	1.37	86.68	1.37	86.34
Annual Average	239678.67	11.68	11.88	49.24	0.81	88.32	0.81	89.65
2. Sisringa (Population : 3000)								
1994-95	123886	5.36	5.43	1.54	0	94.64	0	95.87
1995-96	107911	8.54	11.22	19.91	1.01	91.46	1.33	120.21
1996-97	207665	7.69	7.69	3.19	1.27	92.31	1.27	92.3
1997-98	254218	2.76	2.75	0	0.43	97.24	0.42	96.56
Annual Average	173420	6.09	6.77	6.16	0.68	93.91	0.76	101.24
3. Kedar (Population: 1743)								
1995-96	163973	14.13	14.26	0	0.49	85.87	0.5	86.64
1996-97	307211	7.83	7.61	0	0.51	92.17	0.5	89.65
1997-98	199087	15.02	14.16	0	0.56	84.98	0.53	80.12
Annual Average	223423.67	12.33	12.01	0	0.52	87.67	0.51	85.47
4. Kanakbira (Population : 1551)								
1995-96	72931	15.82	20.04	2.05	2.35	84.18	2.98	106.64
1996-97	139601	11.75	11.88	12.3	0.99	88.25	1.01	89.3
1997-98	493911	3.46	331	3.52	0.29	96.54	0.27	92.36
Annual Average	235481	10.34	11.74	5.96	1.21	89.66	1.42	96.10

Table 3.4 : Per Capita Income and Expenditure of Sample Gram Panchayats

(In Rupees)

	Village Panchayat Year	Tax	Internal Re-sources	Assigned Revenue	Grants	Receipts	Expen-diture
1.	**Kedkela**						
	1994-95	—	—	—	—	—	—
	1995-96	—	—	—	—	—	—
	1996-97	1.54	7.92	0.90	75.49	84.31	85.54
	1997-98	7.94	15.13	0	81.97	122.78	115.36
2.	**Sisringa**						
	1994-95	0.03	2.24	0	39.59	41.83	41.29
	1995-96	0.8	4.03	0.48	42.76	47.27	35.97
	1996-97	0.17	5.32	0.88	63.01	69.21	69.22
	1997-98	0	2.32	0.36	81.47	84.15	84.73
3.	**Kedar**						
	1994-95	—	—	—	—	—	—
	1995-96	0	1.34	0.47	81.03	94.91	94.07
	1996-97	0	13.41	0.88	157.15	171.44	176.25
	1997-98	0	16.17	0.60	90.91	107.68	114.22
4.	**Kanakbira**						
	1994-95	—	—	—	—	—	—
	1995-96	0.19	9.42	1.40	48.74	59.56	47.02
	1996-97	1.31	10.69	0.90	79.47	91.06	90
	1997-98	0.37	10.53	0.87	264.81	304.66	318.44

Source : Commissioner of Panchayats, Government of Madhya Pradesh.

the taxable items assigned to Gram Panchayats. It was reported by one sample Gram Panchayat (Sisringa) that they have imposed profession tax, as there are several shops under its jurisdiction. They expressed inability in collection of tax amount because those shopkeepers are not ready to pay profession tax on the plea that they are already paying sales tax to the government so why should they pay the profession tax; and how many taxes they will pay. The local leaders are not in a position to convince the prospective taxpayers that sales tax is entirely different than profession tax. Moreover, they dot not have any enforcement machinery to realise the tax amount. The plausible way to tackle this situation would be: as the Gram Panchayat imposed the profession tax by passing a resolution from the general body of the Gram Panchayat, instead, had it been discussed in the Gram Sabha prior to passing the resolution, people would have arrived at the consensus on this issue. As all villagers would have been a party to this decision, hence it would have facilitated the Gram Panchayat to realise its move.

It was also reported by the sample Gram Panchayats that they have increased the rate of house tax from Rs.2 to Rs.5, only few persons have deposited the enhanced amount, now they have to pursue people to pay it. Usually, people pay taxes at the time of election when the contesting candidate for each ward is persuaded to collect taxes within his jurisdiction. Though Gram Panchayats do maintain record of taxpayers and arrears amount due with each taxpayer, due to inadequate staff position in the Gram Panchayat, tax amount is not completely realised.

The reason for the higher tax collection of one sample Gram Panchayat (Kedkela) was the personal efforts of the Sarpanch. The Sarpanch of this Gram Panchayat pointed out that he has taken initiative and interest in mobilising tax revenue. The efforts in this direction were to increase the tax amount of house tax, collection of arrears of street light, collection from Kanzi house and imposition of profession tax. It is a pointer for other Gram Panchayats that if local leaders take special effort and initiative then they could realise the goal.

Janpad Panchayat

The tax revenue of Janpad Panchayat is mainly from entertainment tax. The other tax source is the development tax on agriculture land, which is not realised by any Janpad Panchayat. Table 3.5 provides data pertaining to total receipts of Janpad Panchayats of the State for six-year period. It shows that collection of revenue from taxes is only from entertainment tax. The per capita income from this source is less than Rupee one, which is not significant, and it has fluctuating trend. Despite the increase in the rates in 1996, increase in revenue collection from this source has not increased much, as expected. In rural areas in the State, such entertainment

Table 3.5 : Receipts of Janpad Panchayats of Madhya Pradesh

S.No	Items	1992-93		1993-94		1994-95		1995-96		1996-97		1997-98	
		Amount	PC	Amount	PC	Amount	PC	Amount	PC	Amount	PC	Amount	PC
(1)	(2)	(3)	(4)	(5)	(6)	(7)	(8)	(9)	(10)	(11)	(12)	(13)	(14)
A.	**Taxes**												
(i)	Entertainment	2227	—	11016	—	9311	—	16802	—	16346	—	16507	—
	Sub-Total (A)	2227	0.06	11016	0.32	9311	0.27	16802	0.48	16346	0.47	16507	0.47
B.	**Non-Tax Revenue/User Charges**												
(i)	Fairs and Festivals	1349	—	4631	—	5439	—	7207	—	8292	—	8374	—
(ii)	Fishery	—	—	473	—	773	—	2159	—	2202	—	2246	—
(iii)	Ferry Service	2445	—	4467	—	6955	—	18594	—	15004	—	15754	—
(iv)	Obligatory Services (Education)	—	—	—	—	—	—	—	—	452019	—	1839204	—
(v)	Interest on Deposit Money	13203	—	18202	—	17975	—	18887	—	19075	—	19265	—
	Sub-Total (B)	16997	—	27773	—	31142	—	46847	—	496592	—	1884843	—
C.	**Assigned Revenue**												
(i)	Surcharge on Stamp Duty	90073	—	118703	—	126262	—	126262	—	144426	—	181097	—
(ii)	Local Cess on Land Revenue	1520	—	1520	—	1520	—	1520	—	—	—	—	—
(iii)	Mines and Minerals	—	—	—	—	—	—	641	—	705	—	775	—
(iv)	Land Revenue	7500	—	7500	—	7500	—	7500	—	—	—	—	—
	Sub-Total (C)	99093	—	127723	—	135282	—	135923	—	145131	—	181872	—

(Contd.)

Table 3.5 (*Contd.*)

(1)	(2)	(3)	(4)	(5)	(6)	(7)	(8)	(9)	(10)	(11)	(12)	(13)	(14)
D.	**Grants-in-Aid (State)**												
(i)	General Purpose Grant	—	—	—	—	—	—	—	—	—	—	—	—
(ii)	Specific Purpose Grant (Honorarium)	—	—	—	—	—	—	51381	—	54380	—	55575	—
(iii)	Grant for Development Purpose	—	—	—	—	—	—	—	—	—	—	242507	—
	Sub-Total (D)	—	—	—	—	—	—	51381	—	54380	—	298082	—
E.	**TFC Grants**	—	—	—	—	—	—	—	—	70000	—	70000	—
F.	**Centrally Sponsored Schemes**	—	—	—	—	—	—	—	—	—	—	955263	—
	(15% of JRY)	—	—	—	—	—	—	—	—	—	—	—	—
G.	**Others (Adm. Exp. Transferred from Zilla Panchayat)**	—	—	—	—	—	—	485	—	297	—	392	—
	Sub-Total (E+F+G)	—	—	—	—	—	—	485	—	70297	—	1025655	—
	Grand Total	118317	—	166512	—	175735	—	251438	—	782746	—	3406959	—

Amount (Rs. Thousands) PC = Per Capita (Rupees)

Source : Commissioner of Panchayats, Government of Madhya Pradesh.

Table 3.6 : Abstract of Receipts and Expendiure of Janpad Panchayats

S.No	Items	1992-93	1993-94	% of increase	1994-95	% of increase	1995-96	% of increase	1996-97	% of increase	1997-98
1.	Tax Revenue	2227	11016	394.7	9311	-15.5	16802	80.5	16346	-2.7	16507
	% of Total	1.88	6.62		5.30		6.68		2.09		0.48
2.	Non-Tax Revenue	16997	27773	63.4	31142	12.1	46847	50.4	496592	960.0	1884843
	% of Total	14.37	16.68		17.72		18.63		63.44		55.32
3.	Assigned Revenue	99093	127723	28.9	135282	5.9	135923	0.5	145131	6.8	181872
	% of Total	83.75	76.70		76.98		54.06		18.54		5.34
4.	Grants-in-Aid	—	—		—		51381		54380	5.8	298082
	% of Total						20.43		6.95		8.75
5.	TFC & Centrally Sponsored Schemes	—	—		—		485		70297	14394.2	1025655
	% of Total						0.19		8.98	93.69	30.10
	Total	118317	166512	486.95	175735	2.57	251438	131.36	782746	15364.15	3406959
	Total Expenditure	100652	129629	28.79	136101	4.99	202184	48.55	806377	298.83	3409192

Source : Commissioner of Panchayats, Government of Madhya Pradesh.

performance is not static, it is occasional in nature, and hence income from this source is not assured. Table 3.6 shows that the percentage increase in income for this source is fluctuating and contribution of tax revenue to total receipt of Janpad Panchayats is between 1 to 6 per cent. In sample Janpad Panchayats, the income from this source is not encouraging. Table 3.7 shows that annual average tax income of sample Janpad varies between three to six thousand, which is not significant. The annual average percentage of tax income to the total internal resources of sample Janpads is 1 per cent to 5 per cent. The per capita tax revenue for sample Janpad Panchayats (Table 3.8) is quite low and negligible. Thus, these bodies do not have assured and significant income from tax sources rather it is quite low.

Zilla Panchayat

As stated above, Zilla Panchayats do not have any tax revenue sources. Hence, data pertaining to Zilla Panchayats in Tables 3.9, 3.10 and 3.11 do not show any figure with respect to tax revenue.

Non-Tax Revenues

The non-tax revenues are another important source of internal resources of these bodies. The items under non-tax sources are already mentioned above.

In respect of non-tax revenues of Gram Panchayats, it has good number of items to mobilise resources and has better scope as compared to tax sources. It can be seen in Table 3.1 that there are ten items listed and data (six year) reveals that the per capita income is increasing and it has reached to about Rupees five in 1997-98. The per capita income from this source is about double than tax revenue. Among the items of non-tax sources available with Gram Panchayats, the contribution is more from fees, market rate, ferry services and kanji house. Table 3.2 shows that the share

Table 3.7 : Composition of Resources of Sample Janpad Panchayats

Year	Internal Tax	Re-source Non-tax	Total (2+3)	Assigned Revenue	Grant-in-aid others	Invest-ment/ Loans realised	Total (5+6)	Total (4+8)	Grand Total of Receipts
(1)	(2)	(3)	(4)	(5)	(6)	(7)	(8)	(9)	(10)
1. Dharmjaygarh (Population : 142652)									
1994-95	3610	56889	60499	333760	873817	1930	1207577	1268076	1270006
1995-96	445	76747	77192	385565	1024092	930	1409657	1486849	1487779
1996-97	1520	254496	256016	360415	1270600	360	1631015	1887031	1887391
1997-98 (BE)	5000	1770500	1775500	415000	2592800	2000	3007800	4783300	4785300
1998-99 (BE)	5000	1370500	1375500	500000	4096800	2000	4596800	5972300	5974300
Annual Average	3115	705826.4	708941	398948	1971621.8	1444	2370570	3079511	3080955.2
2. Sarangarh (Population : 153382)									
1994-95	2130	35270	37400	334790	5634720	300000	898510	935910	1235910
1995-96	700	64060	64760	408520	1788150	270000	2196670	2261430	2531430
1996-97	22000	57750	79750	386350	7383090	832000	7769440	7849190	8681190
1997-98	0	38570	38570	0	17636929	0	1763929	17675499	17675499
1998-99 (upto Nov. 99)	8000	90000	98000	425000	5727466	440000	6152466	6250466	6690466
Annual Average	6566	57130	63696	310932	6619871	368400	6930803	6994499	7362899

Source : Respective Janpad Panchayats.

(Contd.)

Table 3.7 *(Contd.)*

Year	Total Expen-diture Col.10	Col.4 as % of Col 10	Col.4 as % of Col. 11	Col.2 as % of Col. 4	Col.5 as % of Col.10	Col.6 as % of Col.10	Col. 8 as % of Col.10	Col. 5 as % of Col.11	Col. 6 as % of Col.11	Col.8 as % of Col 11	Col.9 as % of Col. 11
(1)	(11)	(12)	(13)	(14)	(15)	(16)	(17)	(18)	(19)	(20)	(21)
1. Dharmjaygarh (Population : 142652)											
1994-95	822681	4.76	7.35	5.97	26.28	68.8	95.08	40.57	106.22	146.79	154.14
1995-96	1323092	5.19	5.83	0.58	25.92	68.83	94.75	29.14	77.4	106.54	112.38
1996-97	2249964	13.56	11.38	0.59	19.1	67.32	86.42	16.02	56.47	72.49	83.87
1997-98 (BE)	4407780	37.1	40.28	0.28	8.67	54.18	62.85	9.42	58.82	68.24	108.52
1998-99 (BE)	5753595	23.02	23.91	0.36	8.37	68.57	76.94	8.69	71.2	79.89	103.8
Annual Average	2911422.4	16.726	17.75	1.556	17.668	65.54	83.208	20.768	74.02	94.79	112.54
2. Sarangarh (Population : 153382)											
1994-95	1774630	3.03	2.11	5.7	27.09	45.61	72.7	18.87	31.77	50.63	52.74
1995-96	2382890	2.56	2.72	1.08	16.14	70.64	86.78	17.14	75.04	92.19	94.9
1996-97	7835130	0.92	1.02	27.59	4.45	85.05	89.5	4.93	94.23	99.16	100.18
1997-98	7868017	0.22	0.49	0	0	99.78	99.78	0	224.16	224.16	224.65
1998-99 (upto Nov. 99)	4296479	1.46	2.28	8.16	6.35	85.61	91.96	9.89	133.31	143.2	145.48
Annual Average	4831429.2	1.638	1.724	8.506	10.806	77.338	88.144	10.166	111.7	121.87	123.59

Table 3.8 : Per Capita Income and Expenditure of Sample Janpad Panchayats

(In Rupees)

Year	Tax	Internal Resources	Assigned Revenue	Grants	Total Receipts	Expenditure
			Dharmjaygarh			
1994-95	0.02	0.42	2.33	6.12	8.9	5.76
1995-96	0.003	0.54	2.7	7.17	10.42	9.27
1996-97	0.01	1.79	2.52	8.9	13.23	15.77
1997-98	0.03	12.44	2.9	18.17	33.54	30.89
1998-99	0.03	9.64	3.5	28.71	41.88	40.33
			Sarangarh			
1994-95	0.01	0.24	2.18	3.67	8.05	11.57
1995-96	0.004	0.42	2.66	11.65	16.5	15.53
1996-97	0.14	0.51	2.51	48.13	56.59	51.08
1997-98	0	0.26	0	114.98	115.23	51.29
1998-99	0.05	0.63	2.77	37.34	43.61	28.01

Source : Commissioner of Panchayats, Government of Madhya Pradesh.

of non-tax revenue to the total receipts of the Gram Panchayats varies between 3 to 6 per cent which is more than the tax income. The percentage increase in the revenue from this source is showing increasing trend. In the sample Gram Panchayats (Table 3.3), the annual average income from this source ranges from ten to twenty-five thousand rupees, which is reasonable as compared to tax revenue.

While analysing the data on non-tax revenues of sample Gram Panchayats, the State Finance Commission found that 11 per cent Gram Panchayats mobilise resources from market fee and 15 per cent from registration of cattle. Moreover, there has been increase in the number of Gram Panchayats collecting fees from items assigned to them and resources are mobilised from non-tax sources particularly after the 73rd Amendment period. Another important area for raising income is from water bodies. In the State, invariably all districts have water bodies through which they earn ferry rent or leasing tanks for fisheries activities. As Gram Panchayats are vested with the powers to lease out tanks below 10 hectare, this has good scope to raise revenues. In leasing out fisheries ponds, sample Gram Panchayats (GPs) reported that recovery of lease amount is difficult. According to the latest government notification, they have to lease out for ten years period and it cannot be cancelled within the lease period even in case of non-payment of lease amount. Earlier GPs were leasing out for three years but now it has to be leased out for enhanced period of ten years. Thus, it has restricted their autonomy, loss in income and they have to suffer.

Janpad Panchayat

The revenues augmented by Janpad Panchayats are generally from ferry services, leasing out fisheries ponds, fair and festivals and interest from deposits. The state level data (Table 3.5) shows that non-tax revenue of Janpad Panchayats (JPs) is substantial and more than tax revenue. It shows increasing trend and it has gone up by 760 per cent in 1996-97 (Table 3.6). The trend is highly encouraging. The per cent share of non-tax revenue to total receipts of Janpad has gone up to 63 per cent which is substantial.

Among the non-tax revenue sources, the contribution from interest on deposits is highest than any other item. In the sample Janpad Panchayats also, Dharamjaygarh was receiving very high income from interest on deposits and from auction of ferry ghat. Table 3.7 shows that sample Janpads have higher income from non-tax revenues than tax. As also, the non-tax income in sample Janpads shows increasing trend. In one sample Janpad (Sarangarh), realisation of non-tax revenues is not regular because it is predominantly tribal area. They are not imposing any fine or penalty on encroachment. This power is unutilised. Remarkably, the annual average income from this source is more than 7 lakh in Dharamjaygarh whereas in Sarangarh it is only 57 thousand.

Evidently, income from fairs and festivals has limited scope and it cannot be a regular income source. The new dispensation has been empowered to lease out fisheries ponds having an average area of 10-100 hectares. If it is properly harnessed and exploited, it can give better income. Also, the ferry services have better scope to increase income provided it is auctioned objectively, without any motive.

One sample Janpad reported that they are planning to construct houses out of their available own resources and it will be given to the staff members on rental basis. This will serve two purposes; staff will get accommodation, and in turn, JP will have regular income from rent.

Zilla Panchayat

Generally, Zilla Panchayat has income from non-tax sources. Among them, the items, which are very common, are rent from fisheries, rent from properties and interest from deposits. The data pertaining to non-tax revenue for all Zilla Panchayats (ZPs) of State shows (Table 3.10) that the per capita income from this source has increased from 0.07 paisa to Rs.2.69 during 1992-93 to 1997-98.

The new dispensation of Zilla Panchayats has been empowered to lease out fisheries tank with average water spread of more than 100 to 2000 hectares. This is new source of income with good scope provided it is properly utilised. Now, ZPs are also getting administrative service charges from DRDA from 1995-96.

Table 3.11 shows that percentage increase in non-tax revenue is fluctuating and it shows negative growth in 1994-95 whereas in subsequent year it has steep increase by 354 per cent. The contribution of non-tax revenue to the total receipts of ZPs varies from 2 per cent to 11 per cent. It is also evident that they are heavily dependent upon grants hence per cent contribution from non-tax income is quite low.

The sample Zilla Panchayat does not have any income from non-tax sources (Table 3.9). The ZP has no water tank under them so they do not get any income and they have no such properties vested with them to earn income.

So far the mobilisation of internal resources are concerned, the performance of these bodies are not up to the expectations.

Table 3.9 : Composition of Resources of Zilla Panchayat : Raigarh

(Popularion : 1559232)

Receipts

(In Rs.)

Year	General Purpose Grants	Specific Purpose Grants	Tenth Finance Commission	JRY	Family Benefit	Maternity Benefit	Old Age Pension	Balika Samrudhi	Health	Total
(1)	(2)	(3)	(4)	(5)	(6)	(7)	(8)	(9)	(10)	(11)
1994-95	—	—	—	121309000	—	—	—	—	—	121309000
1995-96	—	—	—	148723000	2120000	1193000	3465000	—	—	155501000
1996-97	—	—	—	68666000	2734000	—	9464000	—	4337000	85201000
1997-98	555550	—	25560000	74020000	11380000	988000	18708000	200000	679900	132091450
1998-99	497777	204794	25190000	70607000	6396000	2287000	11933000	1686500	448000	119250071
Annual Average	526663.5	204794	25375000	96665000	5657500	1489333.3	10892500	943250	1821633.3	122670504

Expenditure

Year	Tenth Finance Commission	Salary of Panchayat Staff	Salary of Teachers	Salary of Health Staff	Family Benefit	Maternity Benefit	Old age Pension	Balika Samrudhi	EAS	Total
(1)	(2)	(3)	(4)	(5)	(6)	(7)	(8)	(9)	(10)	(11)
1994-95	—	220800	—	—	—	—	—	—	130251200	130472000
1995-96	—	211700	490000	—	335500	—	—	—	151100000	152137200
1996-97	—	214000	650000	264800	4357000	1129000	8750000	—	132644800	148009600
1997-98	24360000	230000	2280000	605000	9683000	960000	14493000	180000	148191400	200982400
1998-99	25105000	268700	28441000	598600	9909000	2378600	12885000	1702500	131517100	212805500
Annual Average	24732500	229040	7965250	489466.6667	6071125	1489200	12042667	941250	138740900	168881340

Source : Raigarh Zilla Panchayat.

Table 3.10 : Receipts of Zilla Panchayats of Madhya Pradesh

S.No	Items	1992-93		1993-94		1994-95		1995-96		1996-97		1997-98	
		Amount	PC	Amount	PC	Amount	PC	Amount	PC	Amount	PC	Amount	PC
(1)	(2)	(3)	(4)	(5)	(6)	(7)	(8)	(9)	(10)	(11)	(12)	(13)	(14)
A.	**Non-Tax Revenue**												
(i)	Fishery Rental	—	—	538	0.01	834	0.01	2320	0.04	2366	0.04	2413	0.04
(ii)	Any other fees Property Rent Other	1223	0.02	537	0.01	478	0.01	1282	0.02	3131	0.05	3265	0.06
(iii)	Administrative Service Charges (DRDA)							14506	0.26	20867	0.36	145977	2.47
(iv)	Interest on Deposit Money	2448	0.05	4178	0.08	3760	0.07	4934	0.09	7652	0.13	7729	0.13
	Sub-Total (A)	3671	0.07	5253		5072	0.09	23042	0.41	34016	0.59	159384	2.69
B.	**Assigned Revenue**												
(i)	Mines and Minerals	—	—	—	—	—	—	—	—	59213	1.02	59213	1.00
(ii)	Land Revenue	7500	0.14	7500	0.14	7500	0.13	7500	0.13	—	—	—	—
	Sub-Total (B)	7500	0.14	7500	0.14	7500	0.13	7500	0.13	59213	1.02	59213	1.00
C.	**Grants-in-Aid from State**												
(i)	General Purpose Grant	—	—	—	—	—	—	—	—	13567	0.23	15000	0.25
(ii)	Specific Purpose Grant Honorarium, Training, etc.	2477	0.05	3343	0.06	4956	0.09	32914	0.58	32722	0.56	31247	0.53
(iii)	Grant for Development Purpose	30000	0.56	30000	0.55	30000	0.54	212267	3.73	1114777	19.22	1809583	30.58

(*Contd.*)

Table 3.10 (*Contd.*)

(1)	(2)	(3)	(4)	(5)	(6)	(7)	(8)	(9)	(10)	(11)	(12)	(13)	(14)
D.	**TFC Grants**	—	—	—	—	—	—	—	—	30000	0.52	30000	0.51
E.	**Centrally Sponsored Schemes**												
(i)	Central	—	—	—	—	—	—	—	—	—	—	3630824	61.35
(ii)	State	—	—	—	—	—	—	—	—	—	—	1295618	21.89
(iii)	National Old Age Pension	—	—	—	—	—	—	261608	4.60	504243	8.69	450604	7.61
(iv)	National Maternity Benefit Schemes	—	—	—	—	—	—	34804	0.61	29722	0.51	39193	0.66
F.	**Others** health worker-Central	—	—	—	—	—	—	—	—	—	—	14740	0.25
	State	—	—	—	—	—	—	—	—	—	—	23515	0.40
	Total (C + D + E + F)	32477	0.61	33343	0.61	34956	0.63	541593	9.53	1725031	29.74	7340324	124.03
	Grand Total	43648	0.82	46096	0.84	47528	0.85	572135	10.07	1818260	31.35	7558921	127.72

Amount (Rs. Thousands) PC = Per Capita (Rupees)
Source : Commissioner of Panchayats, Government of Madhya Pradesh.

Table 3.11 : Abstract of Receipts and Expendiure of Zilla Panchayats

(Rs. Thousands)

S.No	Items	1992-93	1993-94	% of increase	1994-95	% of increase	1995-96	% of increase	1996-97	% of increase	1997-98
1.	Non-Tax Revenue	3671	5253	43.1	5072	-3.4	23042	354.3	34016	47.6	159384
	% of Total	8.41	11.40		10.67		4.03		1.87		2.11
2.	Assigned Revenue	7500	7500	0.0	7500	0.0	7500	0.0	59213	689.5	59213
	% of Total	17.18	16.27		15.78		1.31		3.26		0.78
3.	Grants-in-Aid	32477	33343	2.7	34956	4.8	245181	601.4	1161066	373.6	1855830
	% of Total	74.41	72.33		73.55		42.85		63.86		24.55
4.	TFC & Centrally Sponsored Schemes	—	—	—	—	—	296412		563965	90.3	5484494
	% of Total	—	—	—	—	—	51.81		31.02		72.56
	Total Receipts	43648	46096	45.76	47528	1.4	572135	955.7	1818260	1201.0	7558921
	Total Expenditure	43829	46984	7.20	47740	1.61	565544	1084.63	1749180	209.29	7366897

Source : Commissioner of Panchayats, Government of Madhya Pradesh.

For Gram Panchayats, it constitutes about five to seven per cent of their total receipts. In sample GPs, the annual average per cent of internal resources to total receipt is 6 per cent to 12 per cent (Table 3.1, Col.12), which is higher than the State level. The Graph 6 shows that the contributions of own income to total receipt is 30 per cent to 15 per cent for sample GPs. Table 3.4 shows that the per capita internal resources of sample GPs fluctuates between Rs.15 to Rs.2. For Janpad Panchayats, the internal resources constitute minimum 16 per cent to maximum 65 per cent. In sample JPs, the annual average of internal resources is 16 per cent and the per capita average varies from 24 paisa to Rs.12, which is insignificant. For ZPs, the highest share of own revenue to the total receipt is 11 per cent but it has subsequently decreased to 2 per cent because of higher allocation of grants to these bodies in recent years. In fine, the above discussions on available data and field observations, it is indicative that Gram Panchayats are not properly utilising either obligatory or optional sources of tax and non-tax revenues. The reasons are inadequacy of staff and their proficiency, non-availability of requisite infrastructure and lack of initiative by local leaders and their will to do so. Besides, Gram Sabha is not activated to use it as a forum for building up awareness among villagers regarding crucial issues of finances so that full support of people can be enlisted in these matters. As also, there is no effort by the government to assess the resources of low tax yield and suggest suitable measures to these bodies.

The State Finance Commission has also observed that Gram Panchayats have not been able to exploit to optimum level even obligatory taxes entrusted to them. The helplessness is due to various reasons. It is mainly because of inadequacy of staff for collection of revenue, lack of sufficient support of people, non-availability of rules published by the government with regard to imposition and collection of specific taxes, etc. It is also because of indifference, ignorance, fear of adverse public relation and unpopularity of local leaders.

Measures Required for Better Local Revenue Mobilisation

The plausible measures needed to improve the financial situation of panchayats on the basis of identified problems are given below. These measures will have direct bearing upon the mobilisation performance, if it is considered for future action.

Local leaders of panchayats as well as functionaries responsible for finances should have better understanding of financial powers and fully acquainted with rules/regulations to raise resources within their purview. Undoubtedly, finance is becoming increasingly complicated technical subject and particularly the elected representatives would find it difficult to appreciate the implications on the financial structure of panchayats. Therefore, a specific sensitisation programme focusing financial matters should be introduced for all functionaries.

Another important aspect is to activate Gram Sabha and use it as a forum to build awareness among people, especially in the matters relating to taxes, payment of taxes, etc. Once awareness is built towards appreciation for value of money and imperatives of development, then, people will cooperate and proverbial attitude not to pay taxes will definitely reduce. This will facilitate in the revenue mobilisation endeavour.

Finance being so central to policy-making process, the Standing Committees established at each level has to play a pivotal role, which is not coming forth now. A serious effort is required to make these bodies effective to meet the expected task in all financial matters.

The newly appointed 'Panchayat Karmi' at the Gram Panchayat level should be made responsible for collection of taxes and non-tax revenues. Alternatively, it may be privatised and task may be assigned to a local person on commission basis, as experienced elsewhere.

Levying of new tax items from obligatory and optional items much depends upon the quality of services rendered by these bodies. People may be ready to pay taxes if services are prompt and of good quality. Therefore, upgradation of infrastructure facilities and quality service is needed. Among the new tax avenues to augment resources. Mandi tax has better prospects. It may be considered for levying.

For improving better infrastructure facilities, various grants like TFC, SFC grants should be properly utilised to develop rural areas. And, these grants may be given as untied funds so that they enjoy freedom in utilising on the basis of local needs and requirements.

Revision of rates of tax and non-tax items should be done objectively, without any motive. These bodies may be given autonomy in these matters. Periodic assessment of taxes should be adhered to.

To streamline and tone up the tax administration, EDP would be the appropriate answer. It is essential to open a cell exclusively to deal with this matter at Janpad or Zilla Panchayat level with computer facilities. This unit will monitor and review all aspects of taxation and accordingly instructions could be given to lower units for timely action and thereby achievements.

Enforcement powers should be vested with the Zilla Panchayat to tackle tax evaders. This will facilitate quick action against evaders. Tax evaders should be exposed in the Gram Sabha meetings.

A scheme of incentive may be introduced for such panchayats who collect cent per cent revenue.

These measures may help revenue raising capacity of panchayats, and thus, financial position may improve.

As stated above, in this chapter, we have restricted our discussions to own sources of revenues of panchayats. Other sources of revenues, such as, assigned revenues and grants have been discussed separately in Chapter 4. Apart from own source of revenues, we will also briefly discuss overall trends of expenditure of panchayats so as to examine their fiscal needs and the nature and extent of the services they provide.

Trends and Patterns of Expenditure

When the financial composition of panchayats is analysed, it is essentially required to examine the trends and patterns of expenditure to make it meaningful. Of course, there is limitation of the available data. Hence, the overall financial composition, and conclusions drawn thereon, on the basis of available data may be treated at best only as approximate and tentative. As the data is not available on classified manner on income and expenditure on revenue account, capital account and public account, we have classified according to the available data.

Broadly, we will classify panchayats expenditure into the categories of: (a) General Administration, (b) Expenditure on Services, (c) Expenditure on Development Grants, and (d) Other Expenditures. The per capita expenditure has been calculated on the basis of projected population of the respective year.

Gram Panchayat

Table 3.12 provides broad function-wise expenditure data for Gram Panchayats for six year period, that is, from 1992-93 to 1997-98. Clearly, the expenditure on general administration has registered an increase in absolute terms as also the per capita. The expenditure on this account is more than expenditure on services. In fact, Gram Panchayats are suppose to provide these basic services since it is obligatory on their part. The expenditure on services has also increased over a period of time, but not in the same proportion as for the general administration. The per capita expenditure on administration has increased more than three fold during 1992-93 to 1997-98. It is because of deployment of additional staff at the Gram Panchayat level, as prescribed by the government; and with the increase in the salary of Village Assistant who are permanent staff. The per cent expenditure item-wise is given in Table 3.13.

Table 3.12 : Expenditure of Gram Panchayats of Madhya Pradesh

S.No	Items	1992-93		1993-94		1994-95		1995-96		1996-97		1997-98	
		Amount	PC	Amount	PC	Amount	PC	Amount	PC	Amount	PC	Amount	PC
(1)	(2)	(3)	(4)	(5)	(6)	(7)	(8)	(9)	(10)	(11)	(12)	(13)	(14)
A.	**General Administration**												
(i)	Salary of Panchayat Staff												
	(a) Village Assistant	216322	6.20	328277	9.41	305808	8.77	394139	11.30	525324	15.07	550717	15.79
	(b) Panchayat Staff	26881	0.77	26950	0.77	47336	1.36	66886	1.92	107765	3.09	113153	3.25
	(c) Panchayat Karmi							52900	1.52	123417	3.54	129133	3.70
(ii)	Terminal Benefits	7440	0.21	9920	0.28	12400	0.36	14880	0.43	18619	0.53	22358	0.64
(iii)	Maintenance	22549	0.65	23193	0.67	37317	1.07	42351	1.21	50656	1.45	53189	1.53
	Sub-Total (A)	273192	7.83	388340	11.13	402861	11.56	571156	16.38	825781	23.68	868550	24.91
B.	**Expenditure on Services**												
(i)	Water Supply	22844	0.66	24400	0.70	25299	0.73	81299	2.33	98568	2.83	103496	2.97
(ii)	Street Lighting	16661	0.48	15029	0.43	34755	1.00	41732	1.20	49504	1.42	51979	1.49
(iii)	Education	6639	0.19	15536	0.45	12500	0.36	15755	0.45	24132	0.69	25339	0.73
(iv)	Public Health	725	0.02	2560	0.07	2064	0.06	3622	0.10	6838	0.20	7180	0.21
(v)	Sanitation	5384	0.15	5012	0.14	7266	0.21	6803	0.20	10130	0.29	10637	0.31
(vi)	Roads	75317	2.16	57456	1.65	65544	1.88	53754	1.54	85963	2.47	90261	2.59
(vii)	Others	23817	0.68	27480	0.79	41879	1.20	49541	1.42	89329	2.56	93795	2.69
(viii)	Parks & Play Grounds	6369	0.18	8004	0.23	4387	0.13	7094	0.20	7846	0.23	8238	0.24
(ix)	Library & Reading Room	7334	0.21	6748	0.19	642	0.02	1047	0.03	7947	0.23	8344	0.24
(x)	Markets	3428	0.10	2192	0.06	4448	0.13	11610	0.33	3397	0.10	3567	0.10
(xi)	Bus Stands	4296	0.12	3425	0.10	5880	0.17	7403	0.21	15077	0.43	15831	0.45
	Sub-Total (B)	172814	4.95	167842	4.81	204664	5.89	279660	8.01	398731	11.45	418667	12.02

(*Contd.*)

Table 3.12 : (*Contd.*)

(1)	(2)	(3)	(4)	(5)	(6)	(7)	(8)	(9)	(10)	(11)	(12)	(13)	(14)
C.	**Expenditure on Development Grants**												
(i)	Grant from State Government	76100	2.18	54600	1.57	71200	2.04	80000	2.29	3500	0.10	62527	1.79
(ii)	Specific purpose Grant (G.P.)											1673050	47.98
(iii)	TFC Grants									771700	22.13	771700	22.13
(iv)	Cetrally sponsored schemes State	569531	16.33	490070	14.05	488021	14.00	655758	18.81	313238	8.98	619758	17.77
(v)	Centrally sponsored scheme Central	2007170	57.56	1960279	56.22	1675978	48.06	2554949	73.27	2347416	67.32	2662534	76.36
	Sub-total	2652801	76.07	2504949	71.84	2235199	64.1	3290707	94.37	3435854	98.53	5789569	166.03
	Grand Total	3098807	88.85	3061131	87.78	2842724	81.55	4141523	118.76	4660366	133.66	7076786	202.96

Amount (Rs. Thousands) PC = Per Capita (Rupees)
Source : Commissioner of Panchayats, Government of Madhya Pradesh.

Table 3.13 : Percentage Expenditure of Gram Panchayats

S.No.	Items	1992-93	1993-94	1994-95	1995-96	1996-97	1997-98
1.	General Administration	8.8	12.7	14.2	13.8	17.7	12.3
2.	Expenditure on Services	5.6	5.5	7.2	6.7	8.6	5.9
3.	Expenditure on Development Grants	85.6	81.8	78.6	79.5	73.7	81.8
	Total	100.00	100.00	100.00	100.00	100.00	100.00

Source : Commissioner of Panchayats, Government of Madhya Pradesh.

It shows that expenditure on development grants constitute the highest percentage, but it is fluctuating. It is due to variation in allocation of grants in a particular year, spill over of the expenditure and unspent amount. The per capita expenditure on this account has increased more than two folds during this period (Table 3.12).

The expenditure on essential services like water supply, street lighting, sanitation, education and health has increase steady, but it is still less than the establishment expenditure. A quantum jump in allocation of funds for these services are due to fact that the SFC has recommended devolving funds to Gram Panchayats for basic services from 1995 onwards.

Table 3.2 shows that per cent increase in the total expenditure of Gram Panchayats was negative for two consecutive years but from 1995-96 it has increased by 45 per cent. Clearly, it demonstrates a demarcated trend in the expenditure before 1995-96 and after. As mentioned earlier, it is due to more devolution of funds to panchayats from a large number of developmental activities under various schemes.

In the sample Gram Panchayats, total expenditure of four Gram Panchayats show increasing trend (Table 3.3). The annual average of receipts and expenditures show Gram Panchayats are in surplus except one sample panchayat having deficit (Graph 1). This is because the grants received are not spent in a particular year and it spilled over to another year and therefore the total expenditure is accounted for more than the total receipt. The expenditure from assigned revenues constitutes a very low per cent of total expenditure for sample Gram Panchayats (Table 3.3, Col.17, Graph 4). The maximum per cent of expenditure is from grants and assigned revenues (Col. 18, Table 3.3: Graph 5). The expenditure from own sources of revenue also show increasing trend (Col.13) and annual average varies from 6 to 12 per cent. This is due to regional variation within the district.

Table 3.12 provides per capita expenditure itemwise for six year period for GPs. The maximum per capita expenditure on establishment comes to Rupees 24 in 1997-98 whereas in the same year the expenditure on services is Rupees 12 and on development it is Rs.166, which is highest. The per capita total expenditure shows increasing trend and it has registered maximum in 1997-98 for Rupees 202, which is quite high as compared to other years. It seems that panchayats are showing scanty attention towards services. More developmental expenditure will result in infrastructure development and capital overheads. With proper initiative, they may be able to develop the area and it may improve conditions of living and levels of income of rural people.

Janpad Panchayats

The expenditure data of Janpad Panchayats is presented in Table 3.14. It is evident that there is a steep rise in the expenditure on administration over a period of time. Nevertheless, it always indicates surplus. The expenditure on services has also increased but not as of administration. The salary of staff has gone up due to merger of erstwhile block administration with Janpad. Naturally, the salary and other related components have gone up tremendously. Besides, the payment of salary of Siksha Karmi has been given to Janpad from 1996-97. So far the expenditure on development grants is concerned, Janpads were not involved initially in developmental work

Table 3.14 : Expenditure of Janpad Panchayats of Madhya Pradesh

S.No	Items	1992-93		1993-94		1994-95		1995-96		1996-97		1997-98	
		Amount	PC	Amount	PC	Amount	PC	Amount	PC	Amount	PC	Amount	PC
A.	**General Administration**												
(i)	(a) Salary of Panchayat Staff & other expenditure	88397		111361		112687		114991		188768		207644	
	(b) Salary of Shiksha Karmi									452019		1839204	
(ii)	Terminal Benefits												
(iii)	Maintenance of Assets	1248		1273		1299		1325		1460		1646	
	Others (Administration)	6904		8682		11761		16899		22726		18455	
	Sub-Total (A)	96549	2.77	121316	3.48	125747	3.61	133215	3.82	664973	19.07	2066949	59.28
B.	**Expenditure on Services**												
(i)	Ferry Services	1223		2234		3478		9297		7502		7877	
(ii)	Fair and Festival	1079		3705		4351		5766		6634		6699	
(iii)	Markets, Mela, Exhibition	1801		2374		2525		2525		2888		3622	
	Sub-Total (B)	4103	0.07	8313	0.17	10354	0.22	17588	0.43	17024	0.41	18198	0.42
C.	**Expenditure on Development Grants**												
(i)	Grant from State Government											242507	
(ii)	Centrally Sponsored Schemes (JRY)											955963	
(iii)	TFC Grants									70000		70000	
(iv)	Other Expenditure (Honororium)							51381		54380		55575	
	Sub-Total (C)		0.05		0.07		0.07	51381	1.55	124380	3.65	1324045	38.08
	Grand Total	100652	2.89	129629	3.72	136101	3.9	202184	5.8	806377	23.13	3409192	97.78

Amount (Rs. Thousands) PC = Per Capita (Rupee)

Source : Commissioner of Panchayats, Government of Madhya Pradesh.

but from 1996-97 they are receiving grants under TFC and other State schemes. This component also constitutes the expenditure on honorarium given to office bearers of the Janpad. The total expenditure shows increasing trend (Table 3.6) and it has gone up by 298 per cent in 1996-97, which is quite high as compared to other years, especially in 1994-95 (4.99%).

The per capita expenditure (Table 3.14) also shows increasing trend and the per capita total expenditure in 1997-98 has reached to Rupees 97. The per capita expenditure on establishment has reached maximum to Rs. 59 in 1997-98 which is quite high as compared to service expenditure (less than Re. 1) and development expenditure (Rs. 35). Thus, the Janpads are spending more on establishment than other component of expenditure in terms of per capita expenditure.

In sample Janpad Panchayats, the annual average expenditure is less than the total annual receipts (Graph 8). As seen for the State level performance on expenditure, the expenditure in both sample Janpads is increasing. The per cent expenditure to the total receipts (Table 3.7) is less, that is, they have surplus. But, this situation is misleading so far the financial requirement is concerned. The per cent of total income from assigned revenue and grants to the total expenditure (Table 3.7, Col. 20 & Graph 14) has fluctuations. In case of Dharmjaygarh, it is declining whereas in the other sample Janpad it is increasing. It appears that one sample Janpad is not fully utilising grants for the development purposes, as expected (Graph 13).

Zilla Panchayat

Table 3.15 shows that Zilla Panchayats were not getting development funds earlier and they were only providing water supply services to people. The expenditure on establishment has tremendously increased in absolute terms. The salary of staff has gone up in 1997-98 by two fold as compared to 1992-93. As Zilla Panchayats are now disbursing salary of

Table 3.15 : Expenditure of Zilla Panchayats of Madhya Pradesh

S.No	Items	1992-93		1993-94		1994-95		1995-96		1996-97		1997-98	
		Amount	PC	Amount	PC	Amount	PC	Amount	PC	Amount	PC	Amount	PC
A.	**General Administration**												
(i)	Salary of Panchayat Staff	6081		6715		6772		8124		8758		12304	
(ii)	Salary of Shiksha Karmi									120158		488902	
(iii)	Salary of Health Worker												
	- Central											23515	
	- State											14740	
(iv)	Maintenance of Assets	365		403		406		487		525		738	
(v)	Others	4906		6523		5606		8087		18000		18738	
	Sub-Total (A)	11352	0.33	13641	0.39	12784	0.37	16698	0.048	147441	4.23	558937	16.03
B.	**Expenditure on Obligatory Services**												
(i)	Water Supply (Reserve Fund)	30000		30000		30000		212267		264830		307660	
(ii)	Forest									1425		1425	
(iii)	Public Health									3248		7560	
(iv)	Others (Development Deptt.)									725116		1004036	
	Sub-Total (B)	30000		30000		30000		212267		994619		1320681	
C.	**Expenditure on Development Grants**												
(i)	Grant from State Government (Honorarium Trg.)	2477		3343		4956	0.1	32914	0.65	32722	0.64	31247	
(ii)	Centrally Sponsored Schemes												
	JRY 20% & 15%, IRDP,												
	EAS - State Share											1295618	
	Central Share											3630824	
	National Old Age Pension/NFB							267891	5.27	514082	10.11	459613	
	National Maternity Benefit Schemes							35774		30316		39977	
(iii)	TFC Grants									30000	0.59	30000	
	Sub-Total (C)	2477	0.07	3343	0.1	4956	0.14	336579	9.65	607120	17.41	5487279	157.37
	Grand Total	43829	0.4	46984	0.49	47740	0.51	565544	9.698	1749180	21.64	7366897	173.4

Amount (Rs. Thousands) PC = Per Capita (Rupees)

Source : Commissioner of Panchayats, Government of Madhya Pradesh.

Shiksha Karmi and health workers, the expenditure on establishment from 1996-97 onwards has gone up.

In the area of delivery of services, they were earlier responsible for only water supply, but from 1996-97, they were entrusted with additional responsibility of health and forest work. In the sphere of water supply, the expenditure has gone up very high in 1997-98. This is because of more grants coming for this service. The expenditure on development grants has also increased tremendously because from 1995-96 they are getting various grants for development purposes. Table 3.11 shows the per cent increase in total expenditure. Evidently, it has increased and it has recorded maximum by 1084 per cent in 1995-96, the year from when the allocation of funds is more.

The per capita expenditure on establishment has increased from less than a rupee for 1992-93 to Rupees 16 in 1997-98. The per capita expenditure (Table 3.15) on development grants has also gone up to the maximum by Rs.15. Similarly, the per capita total expenditure has gone up from less than one rupee to Rs.173 in 1997-98. A clear shift in expenditure trend is visible from 1995-96 onwards because of devolution of funds and functions to Zilla Panchayats in the State.

In the sample district Raigarh, the trend is similar in terms of expenditure (Table 3.9). With the increase in the functional responsibilities and devolution of funds, trend is quite obvious. The pattern of expenditure indicates that they are spending more on development works than the delivery of civic services. They are spending more on maternity benefit, old age pension, employment schemes and family benefit schemes. The sample ZP does not have own income so there is no expenditure out of this source.

The foregoing analysis shows that expenditure trend is increasing and the pattern of expenditure has variations in respect of establishment, service delivery and developmental work. It is due to the fact that devolution of functions and funds to the new dispensation of panchayats in the State has taken place remarkably.

4

FINANCIAL DEVOLUTION ON PANCHAYATS

Local governments throughout the world are, by and large, dependent on subvention from the higher levels of government to meet a significant portion of their revenue. Therefore, financial devolution from higher levels of government to lower level is an important aspect of study in the arena of local public finance. The rationale behind inter-governmental transfers are: (a) the dichotomy between the proportion of public expenditure for which local governments are made responsible, and the proportion of tax assigned to them; (b) very often the elastic revenue sources are retained by the higher levels of government, and consequently local bodies are left with inadequate resources, which need to be supplemented so as to enable them to provide required services at the local level; (c) the available tax bases and tax rates of local government restrict their fiscal capacity and therefore a mismatch between the expenditure needs and revenue means; and (d) transfer is necessary to meet regional economic imbalances and upgradation of the existing level of services to ensure a common minimum standard across regions. Thus, in the literature of fiscal federalism inter-governmental transfers are used to correct vertical fiscal imbalances. In India, the State-panchayat fiscal relations are more complex than anywhere in the federal set-up, but it is gradually evolving. In this chapter an attempt has been made to oversee the flow of funds to panchayats from State and Central governments, which is one of the objectives of the study. In doing so, we will also look into various types of funds, criteria for devolution and quantum of funds given to three-tiers of panchayats in the State.

Generally, the mode of fiscal transfers is made in the form of (a) assigned revenue, (b) grants, and (c) loans. In case of panchayats, the first two items usually account for the maximum transfers on the revenue account. We will now examine each mode of transfer prevalent in the State.

Assigned Revenues

One of the forms of fiscal transfer is revenue from tax revenue. In this mode of transfer, some proportion of amount collected from a tax, which is local in nature within the jurisdiction of a local government, is refunded to that local government. A derivation principle of revenue sharing is applicable. The higher level of government deducts collection charges, which is usually a specified percentage of total receipt. Another method to determine tax sharing is compensatory principle, that is, in the form of compensation for the loss of previously existing sources of revenue. The revenue from the taxes that are not local in nature or the remaining taxes of the State government may be distributed on the basis of a formula. In this method, the percentage of revenue transferred will vary from State to State, depending upon devolution of functions to panchayats.

Usually, the land revenue and stamp duties on transfer of property are the two important taxes within the fiscal domain of the State governments which are shared with the panchayats. Besides, there are two other taxes levied and collected by the State governments and the revenue from which is assigned to the panchayats are entertainment tax and profession tax. In Kerala, motor vehicle tax is another tax source that is shared with the local government on compensatory principle. On the basis of the experiences gained so far with regard to sharing of revenues, it was found that the proportion of revenues which becomes available to local bodies remains unchanged overtime. Also, the release of funds according to legitimate share is not exact and timely. Further, the share of local bodies does not seem to be based upon the relative needs and fiscal capacity of each unit. As a result, the panchayats, which are financially better off, get larger funds while economically backward panchayats who deserve more financial assistance get less. It is likely that this type of fiscal transfer may further aggravate the existing regional imbalances. Moreover, the quantum of funds transferred under this mode is generally quite less.

In Madhya Pradesh, assigned revenues to Panchayati Raj Institutions (PRIs) are land revenue, cess on land revenue and extra stamp duty. A detail examination of each item is presented here.

Land Revenue

Land revenue is one of the important and common taxes which is shared with the PRIs. In the State, right from the first Panchayat Act, land revenue and cess on land revenue were assigned to PRIs. As per the December 1962 Rules, 20 per cent of the proceeds of land revenue assessed in a district in the preceding year is kept as revenue fund and the balance is transferred to Gram Panchayats, Janpad Panchayats and Zilla Panchayats in proportion of 60:12:8. The subsequent notification of rules under the Act of 1981, the proportional distribution of shares among these bodies changed to 60:20:20. But this was abolished as per the recommendations of the SFC in 1996.

Under Section 69(2) of 1981 Act, a provision was made that the State government will withdraw from the consolidated fund of the State an amount equivalent to the proceeds of the cess assessed and proceeds of extra stamp duty realised by it in the preceding financial year and it will be credited in a separate fund called the Madhya Pradesh Panchayat Land Revenue Cess and Stamp Duty Fund. Further, the 1981 Act provides that after due appropriation an amount equal to the land revenue assessed in the State in the previous year be credited in the same fund. This section was amended in November 1984, and the amendment provided that in the financial year 1984-85 an amount of Rs. 750 lakh will be deposited in this fund by the government. An additional amount to the extent of 5 per cent of the amount credited during 1984-85 was deposited in the next financial year.

As per Section (4) (a) of the Act, 1981 and rules prescribed thereon, all tiers of panchayats are to be paid out of the land revenue amount available in the fund as grants. All Janpad Panchayats are paid only out of the amount released from stamp duty [Section (4)(b)]. Another provision in the Act under Section 67(4)(c) provides for share to be paid to Janpad and Gram Panchayat from and out of the amount in the cess fund. In the 1990 Act, no such specific provision was given regarding land revenue amount to be credited in the fund.

In MPPA 1993, similar arrangement has been made for transfer of funds to panchayats. The Section 76 of the 1993 Act does specify the amount of land revenue to be credited by the government in the fund. The provision is similar to 1990 Act which says that an amount equivalent to the land revenue collected during the preceding financial year be credited in the fund by the government to be paid as grant-in-aid to panchayats. In the 1993 Act, 'MP Panchayat Land Revenue Cess on Land Revenue and Stamp Duty Fund' has been renamed as 'MP Panchayati Raj Fund', however.

The provisions of Section 76 of the MPPA, 1993 was further amended in 1996 and notified in January 1997 by substituting it with new Section 76 and Section 76-A(i). This provides for a separate fund named as 'District Panchayati Raj Fund', made available at district level in which proceeds of land revenue, cess on land revenue, other taxes, duties, tolls, fees, etc., after deducting collection charges are credited. Further more, as per section 76-A(i), land revenue and cess realised from a Gram Panchayat area shall be transferred to the said Gram Panchayat every year.

Only Gram Panchayats are recipient of proceeds of land revenue and cess on land revenue after deducting the collection charges by revenue department. This arrangement is unlike earlier where Janpad and Zilla Panchayats were also getting a share. In the new arrangement, these two units do not get any share.

Cess on Land Revenue

Under Section 157(i) of the 1962 Act, Janpad Panchayat was empowered to levy cess on land revenue at the rate of fifteen paise per rupee of land revenue or part thereof exceeding fifty paise assessed. Janpad Panchayat can further raise the rate of cess to the extent of ninety paise. The collected amount of cess was distributed among the Janpad Panchayats. and Gram Panchayats within their jurisdiction in the proportion of 3:2. Rules framed in 1982 changed the criteria of distribution of share among Janpad Panchayats and Gram Panchayats in the proportion of 40:60. This system was in practice but it was abolished in 1996 on the recommendation of SFC.

Additional Cess on Land Revenue

In 1996, the Panchayat Act was further amended and Zilla Panchayat was empowered to increase cess upto Rs.10 for each rupee of land revenue. The revenue from increased cess will be credited in the Nidhi and distributed among the Gram Panchayat, Janpad Panchayat and Zilla Panchayat in the proportion of 50:25:25. So far no Zilla Panchayat has exercised this power and hence it is not operational and no income is generated.

Additional Stamp Duty

To strengthen the financial base of the Janpad Panchayats, under Section 68 of the 1981 Act, provided for imposition of additional stamp duty by 1 per cent on the value of the property situated within the block. As per rules framed in December 1982, the amount realised from additional stamp duty every year will be transferred to the Janpad Panchayats.

Royalty from Minor Minerals

Another revenue assigned to the PRIs is share of royalty out of the income from the exploitation of minor minerals. In the Pre-73rd Amendment period, no such revenue was assigned to the PRIs but after the amendment they were empowered to lease patta for exploitation of mineral sources from mines within their jurisdiction. In this regard, the State government has issued detailed guidelines under Minor Minerals Rules, 1996. Accordingly, the Gram Panchayats, Janpad Panchayats and Zilla Panchayats have been vested with powers to lease quarry/mines of minor minerals like stone, bolders, morrum, grave, sand etc., (listed in Schedule 2 of the Rules) having annual value below Rs. 2.50 lakh, Rs. 2.50 lakh to Rs. 5 lakh and Rs. 5 lakh to Rs. 10 lakh respectively. Revenue from the grant of lease is deposited in the concerned panchayat fund and the share of royalty is distributed among the panchayats as decided by the government. Besides, the share of the proceeds from the royalty of granite mines and others is assigned to the Gram Panchayats and Janpad Panchayats concerned in the State for which they are not empowered to grant lease. As per the order of December 1, 1997 issued by the Mineral Resources Department of Madhya Pradesh under M.P. Minor Mineral Rules, 1996, the following arrangements have been made:

(a) The entire proceeds of the revenue upto Rs. 2.50 lakh to be transferred to the concerned Gram Panchayats.

(b) Where the proceeds of revenue is more than Rs. 2.50 lakhs but less than Rs. 5 lakh, 80 per cent of the amount payable be paid to the concerned Gram Panchayats and the remaining 20 per cent to the concerned Janpad Panchayats.

(c) Where the proceeds of revenue is more than Rs. 5 lakh but less than Rs. 10 lakh, 50 per cent of the amount payable be paid to the concerned Gram Panchayats and the remaining 50 per cent to the concerned Janpad Panchayats.

(d) Where the proceeds of revenue is more than Rs. 10 lakh but less than Rs. 20 lakh, 20 per cent of the amount payable be paid to the concerned Gram Panchayats and the remaining 80 per cent to the concerned Janpad Panchayat.

(e) Where the proceeds of revenue is more than Rs. 20 lakh or where the amount payable is more than Rs. 20 lakh, it will be paid to the concerned Janpad Panchayat.

A condition has been attached that the amount paid to the Janpad Panchayat will be spent for the development of the area of the panchayats where the exploitation of minor minerals is being done.

The SFC has recommended (1996) to discontinue with the existing practice of devolving the share of revenue to the Panchayats from land revenue, cess on land revenue and additional stamp duty. The State government has accepted the recommendation and accordingly decided that under the provisions of the Panchayat Act, land revenue and cess on land revenue be given directly to the Village Panchayats, and the receipts from the additional stamp duty be given to the Janpad Panchayats. Table 4.1 provides the share of assigned revenues given to panchayats in the State. As shown in the table, the increase in share of land revenue from 60 per cent to 100 per cent for Gram Panchayats was introduced in 1995-96 but the actual transfer came into effect from 1997-98.

Rates of Levy

Land Revenue

As per Section 77 of the Madhya Pradesh Land Revenue Code, 1959 (20 of 1959), land revenue or rent is levied on every tenure holder and government lessee in respect of the land held by him in the Gram Panchayat area as per

Table 4.1 : Devolution of Assigned Revenues to Zilla Panchayats

Year	Items	Total Amount (Lakhs)	Share of Rural Local Bodies	Share of Zilla Panchayats
1990-91	Land Revenue	750.00	50%	10%
1991-92	Land Revenue	750.00	50%	10%
1992-93	Land Revenue	750.00	50%	10%
1993-94	Land Revenue	750.00	50%	10%
1994-95	Land Revenue	750.00	50%	10%
1995-96	Land Revenue	750.00	50%	10%
1996-97	Land Revenue	750.00	50%	10%
1997-98	Land Revenue	750.00	50%	10%
1998-99	Additional Cess on land revenue by Zilla Panchayat		100%	25%

Source : Commissioner of Panchayats, Government of Madhya Pradesh.

assessment of rent for different classes of land made by the Settlement Commissioner. The rent fixed by the Settlement Officer varies from plot to plot, area to area and region to region. It also varies for unirrigated and irrigated holdings. Under Section 102 of the Land Revenue Code, 1959, the assessment fixed shall be the land revenue or rent payable annually on such plot number unless modified. Moreover, the assessment fixed under Section 100 of the Land Revenue Code remains valid for a period of thirty years or for a longer period till it is assessed next. The present assessment is more than 30 years and no fresh assessment of land revenue has been done. The rates of land revenue were fixed according to the settlement operation held in 1920s and 1930s in different regions of the State. These rates are still prevalent despite the fact that modernisation in agriculture and agricultural practices has taken place to a great extent which has enabled the farmers to get much more net profit from cultivation at the time of last assessment. In 1974, an attempt was made for updating of land records and a Master Plan of settlement was prepared. Though the settlement operation was carried out in 24 districts and upward revision of Land Revenue was also proposed, the Government did not approve it. Thus, the old rates are still in force. Though frequent revision of rent is not possible, but one possible way would be to evolve a suitable index of agriculture production to increase the rate of land revenue after an interval of at least 5 years. In 1993-94, the average incidence per hectare of land revenue on cultivated area in the State was Rs. 4.45, having a sharp variation from the lowest of 98 paise per hectare in Bastar district to the highest of Rs.13.32 in Ratlam district (Agricultural Statistics of M.P., 1993-94). The reason from Ratlam having high rate is because of the poppy cultivation, which is a cash crop. Though Mandsaur is yet another district where poppy is cultivated, the incidence per acre of land revenue is lower than that of Ratlam. Such anomaly is evident. The districts where mainly food crops are cultivated, the highest rate does not go beyond Rs. 6 per hectare. Under Section 58-A of the M.P. Land Revenue Code, 1959, the payment of land revenue is exempted on uneconomic holdings, *i.e.* upto 5 acres. Under the provisions of sub-section (i) of Section 69 of the 1981 Act, a sum of Rs. 7.50 crore is estimated annually from the land revenue for transfer to the PRIs in the State.

Cess on Land Revenue

In addition to the Land Revenue, the cess on it is also levied. The provision for levying of cess on land revenue is available in the MPPA, 1981 and 1990. Under Section 67 of the MPPA, 1981, cess on Land Revenue be levied for each revenue year on every tenure holder and government lessee in respect of the land held by him in the Gram Panchayat area at the rate of fifty paise per rupee of the Land Revenue on the land. The same provision continues under Section 72 of the 1990 Act as also in sub-section (2) of Section 74 of the 1993 Act.

The rate of cess on land revenue continues to be the same.

Mode of Collection

Land Revenue and Cess on Land Revenue

As per the rules, land revenue is to be paid to the *patel* of village and, where no patel is appointed, to the *patwari* or such other persons as may be authorised to receive land revenue by the State government. If the work of collection of land revenue has been entrusted to a Gram Panchayat or to a Gram Sabha, it is to be paid to such body.

Additional Stamp Duty

The Field Officers of the Inspector General of Registration at the time of registration of documents collect stamp duty. Out of the total amount so realised during a preceding year, the share of panchayats is placed at the disposal of the Directorate of Panchayat by book transfer for further distribution.

Criteria for Distribution

As stated above, the share of Land Revenue, cess on Land Revenue and Additional Stamp Duty are placed at the disposal of the Directorate of Panchayat and Social Welfare for distribution to the PRIs. The State government, as reserve fund, retains 50 per cent of the proceeds of Land Revenue of the preceding year after deducting the collection charges. The remaining 50 per cent are released for distribution in the proportion of 20 per cent, 20 per cent and 60 per cent to Zilla Panchayat, Janpad Panchayat and Gram Panchayats respectively. In the case of Cess on Land Revenue, 40 per cent is distributed to the Janpad Panchayats and the remaining 60 per cent to Gram Panchayats.

The entire amount of the proceeds of additional Stamp Duty is distributed to the Janpad Panchayats. Till 1994-95, the criteria for distribution were the weightage of rural population of the respective units. Now, the per capita amount of the one per cent additional stamp duty is being determined in the proportion of population among Janpad Panchayat of current census.

As mentioned earlier, the criteria for distribution of shares of assigned revenues *i.e.*, Land Revenue, Cess on Land Revenue and Additional Stamp Duty had been changed on the basis of the recommendations of the State Finance Commission. After receiving the sanction order from the State Finance Department, the Directorate of Panchayat and Social Welfare distributes the fund (share of PRIs) to the Chief Executive Office/Collector of the concerned district proportionate to the rural population (1991 Census) of the concerned district. The amount so received by the CEO/ Collector is deposited in the Zilla Panchayat Nidhi. The share of the Zilla Panchayat is retained and the shares of Janpad and Gram Panchayats are transferred to the concerned Janpad Panchayat on the same criteria of population.

Criteria for Inter se Distribution

In order to ensure greater flow of funds to the backward areas as compared to the more prosperous areas, the State Finance Commission calculated the percentage share of each district.

The Commission has recommended the criteria for *inter se* distribution of funds among districts (Table 4A). The suggested parameters are static criteria, poverty indicators and indicators relating to backwardness. The weightage given to each indicator is reasonable, and it is suitable to take care of regional imbalances prevailing within the State.

The criteria for distributing grants among Janpad Panchayat are 70 per cent population, 25 per cent area, and 5 per cent recovery of tax.

The State Finance Commission has recommended that the fund allocated for Gram Panchayats in the districts, the *inter se* distribution for Gram Panchayats in the district will be

Table 4A : Criteria for *inter se* distribution of funds among districts recommended by State Finance Commission

S.No.	Parameters	Weightage (%)
A.	**Static criteria**	
	1. Total Population	21.24
	2. Area	10.625
B.	**Poverty Indicators**	
	3. Rural ST/SC	15
	4. Number of agricultural labourers	10.625
	5. Average gross value of Agricultural Production per hectare	10.625
C.	**Indicators for Backwardness**	
	6. Number of working labourers in the Registered factories per one lakh	10.625
	7. Consumption of electricity per individual	10.625
	8. Literacy rate	10.625

based on the following formula:

Criteria	*Weightage (Per cent)*
Population	75
Area	25

While accepting the recommendation of the SFC, the government has changed the criteria and population is given 70 per cent, area 25 per cent, and tax effort 5 per cent. A new item has been added (tax effort) to ensure that GP should streamline their tax administration.

Periodicity of Release of Funds

Generally, the release of funds to PRIs is not timely. It is observed that the sanction for the release is issued at the end of the financial year or sometimes even after the financial year. Such practice is substantiated by the field data. Moreover, it takes about two months for the Zilla Panchayats to distribute the funds to the Janpad Panchayats and Gram Panchayats within its jurisdiction.

Composition and Trends in Assigned Revenues

Tables 4.1, 4.2 and 4.3 show itemwise share of assigned revenues to Zilla, Janpad and Gram Panchayats respectively for nine-year period from 1990-91 to 1998-99.

As seen in Table 4C, among the four sources of assigned revenues transferred to PRIs in part or full, additional stamp duty constitute the major source of assigned revenue. It is transferred only to Janpad Panchayats. The share of additional stamp duty to the total assigned revenues ranges between minimum of 55.9 per cent in 1997-98 to maximum of 75 per cent in 1994-95. The second major revenue assigned to PRIs is share from land revenue. It constitutes 28.5 per cent of the total assigned revenue in 1992-93 and 23.1 per cent in 1997-98; the exception was in 1996-97 (9.6 per cent) when the due share was not given to Gram Panchayats. Another assigned revenue, started from 1995-96, is royalty from minor minerals. The share from this source was 0.4 per cent in 1995-96, 27.5 per cent in 1996-97 and 19.8 per cent in 1997-98, it shows increasing trend.

In five-year period, the share from land revenue was doubled as it increased from Rs.3.75 crore in 1992-93 to Rs.7.50 crore in 1997-98. The cess on land revenue remained constant at Rs.38 lakh from 1992-93 to 1995-96, declined to Rs.22.80 lakh in 1996-97, regained in 1997-98 to Rs.38 lakh. The decline in 1996-97 was due to discontinuance of payment of shares to Janpad Panchayats and non-payment of due share to the Gram Panchayats. In the initial year 1995-96, the amount of royalty from minor minerals was low to Rs.6.41 lakh because it was the beginning. In subsequent years, it increased to Rs.64.06 lakh in 1996-97 and Rs.64.21 lakh in 1997-98. Evidentially, there has been an increase in the total assigned revenue from Rs.13.14 crore in 1992-93 to Rs.32.41 crore in 1997-98. It is a quantum jump of more than two times. It can, therefore, be said that the flow of funds to panchayats in the State has increased on account of assigned revenues.

Apart from these two-tiers of Panchayat, Zilla Panchayat has been empowered to raise cess on land revenue upto ten times, *i.e.*, upto ten rupees for each rupee of land revenue. But so far no Zilla Panchayat has exercised this power and hence they could not mobilise additional resources available with them.

While examining the functional responsibilities of the three-tiers, the State Finance Commission observed that it is clear from the interpretation of the Act that in the three-tier structure of panchayats, the Janpad and Zilla Panchayats have not been assigned any such obligatory duties for which they are entitled to get the share of taxes. In other words, their functions are limited only as the "agents of the State governments". Therefore, on the basis of SFC recommendations, the share from Land Revenue and Cess on Land Revenue have been discontinued to Zilla Panchayats and Janpad Panchayats, whatever they were getting earlier upto 1994-95. Consequently, on this count, the State government could manage to save Rs.3 crore in 1996-97 and paid to Gram Panchayats only the usual share of Rs.2.48 crore. However, in 1997-98, Gram Panchayats were paid the enhanced shares of land revenue and cess on land revenue amounting to Rs.7.50 crore and Rs.32.80 lakh respectively. Therefore, from 1997-98, the flow of funds to Gram Panchayats has gone up by Rs.3.70 crore per annum, which is an additional transfer of funds from the State to panchayats.

From 1996-97, royalty from minor minerals has become a new source of revenue for panchayats. For the Zilla Panchayats, it is only major assigned revenue. The State is endowed with rich resources of not only major minerals but also minor minerals like stone slabs, sand, gravel, morrum, limestone, slate used for building materials, which has huge potential. As the Panchayats have been delegated with such powers, additional income could be generated out of it. Considering the vast scope of revenues from this source, Panchayats are not properly exploiting it. There are as many as 5899 mines and quarries spread over in 61 districts, which was having an annual income of Rs.8.30 crore earlier. According to a survey conducted by the Mineral Resources Department, it reveals that from April, 1996 to December, 1998 only 3699 lease deeds were executed by the PRIs out of 5899 mines transferred to them. As a result of inaction, the revenue from royalty has fallen approximately by Rs.4.95 crores, which could have otherwise come to panchayats. As reported, only three districts (Narsimhapur, Harda and Indore), out of 61 districts, could increase revenue from minor minerals source whereas in other remaining districts revenue declined. In the study area of this study, no such opportunity was available with the Gram Panchayats. In course of discussion at the State level, it was revealed that some Gram Panchayats are over exploiting minor minerals that may lead to problems in future. Therefore, this aspect needs serious thought while taking any further decision.

Tables 3.10 and 4D reveal a quantum jump in flow of funds from assigned revenue to the Zilla Panchayats. A sum of Rs.75 lakh was being paid annually during 1992-93 to 1995-96, now from 1996-97 onwards it has increased to Rs.5.92 crore. It is because of the revenue transferred out of royalty from minor minerals.

Table 3.5 shows a consistent increase in the share of additional stamp duty assigned to Janpad Panchayats. Taking 1994-95 as the base year for the new dispensation after the 73rd Amendment, it has increased from Rs.12.63 crore to Rs.18.19 crore in 1997-98, per cent increase of 44 per cent. This source of revenue may further increase with the pace of urbanisation depending upon the value of immovable property and transactions.

Similarly, for Gram Panchayats, the trend in the quantum of assigned revenues transferred show an appreciable increase. Table 3.3 shows that the total assigned revenues paid annually during 1992-93 to 1995-96 was Rs.2.47 crore, which has gone up tremendously in 1997-98 by Rs.8.3 crore. The increase is about three-folds and it is due to increase in the land revenue, cess on land revenue and royalty from minor minerals.

Table 4B provides the per capita assigned revenue from different sources given to these bodies. The total per capita assigned revenue from all sources show an increasing trend; it has increased from minimum of Rs.2.77 in 1992-93 to maximum of Rs.6.58 in 1997-98, which is more than two times. For Zilla Panchayat, it has improved from 14 paisa to one rupee, even then it not much significant. In the case of Janpad, it has gone up from Rs.1.91 to Rs.3.20. The increase is more than double. In fact, the per capita assigned revenue for Gram Panchayats remained very meagre throughout for 72 paise. In 1997-98, the per capita assigned revenue has increased by three-folds.

Table 4B : Per Capita Assigned Revenue

Unit of Panchayat	1992-93	1993-94	1994-95	1995-96	1996-97	1997-98
ZP	0.14	0.14	0.13	0.13	1.02	1.00
JP	1.91	2.41	2.50	2.47	2.59	3.20
GP	0.72	0.72	0.72	0.72	0.84	2.38
Total	2.77	3.27	3.35	3.32	4.45	6.58

Per capita (Rupees).

Source: Commissioner of Panchayats, Government of Madhya Pradesh.

Even this increase does not ensure adequacy of funds as the Gram Panchayats have been entrusted to carry out the basic functions of providing services on health and sanitation, conservancy, drinking water resources, roads, street lighting, etc. Though the Janpad Panchayats are not carrying out these obligatory function, the fund position in terms of per capita is better as compared to the Gram Panchayats.

Table 4C reveals that the per capita revenue from additional stamp duty has a consistent increasing trend. It has gone up from Rs.1.73 in 1992-93 to Rs.3.20 in 1997-98, which is about double. The trend of per capita revenue from land revenue shows ups and downs. The minimum was 40 paisa in 1996-97 that increased to the maximum of

Table 4C : Assigned Revenues from Different Sources: Per Capita & Percentage
(Rs. in Thousand)

	Items	1992-93	1993-94	1994-95	1995-96	1996-97	1997-98
1.	Additional	90073	11870	126262	126262	144426	181097
	Stamp	1.73	3	2.34	2.29	2.58	3.20
	duty	(68.6)	2.24	(75.3)	(75.0)	(61.9)	(55.9)
			(74.2)				
2.	Land	37500	37500	37500	37500	22500	75000
	Revenue	0.72	0.70	0.69	0.68	0.40	1.32
		(28.5)	(23.4)	(22.4)	(22.3)	(9.6)	(23.1)
3.	Cess on	3800	3800	3800	3800	2280	3800
	Land	0.07	0.07	0.07	0.07	0.04	0.06
	Revenue	(2.9)	(2.4)	(2.3)	(2.3)	(1.0)	(1.2)
4.	Mines	—	—	—	641	64059	64212
	and				0.01	1.14	1.13
	Minerals				(0.4)	(27.5)	(19.8)
	Total	131373	53170	167562	168203	233265	324109
	Per Capita	2.52	3.01	3.10	3.05	4.16	5.17

Per capita (Rupees).
Note : Figures in parentheses are percentage to total assigned revenues.
Source: Commissioner of Panchayats, Government of Madhya Pradesh.

Rs.1.32 in 1997-98. The annual per capita revenue from cess on land revenue remained 7 paisa upto 1995-96 and declined to 4 paisa in 1996-97 but further recovered to 6 paisa in 1997-98. The revenue yield from this source is not impressive. Though the assignment of revenue from minor minerals was in 1995-96, the annual per capita revenue was one paisa to start with, it has increased to Rs.1.13 in 1997-98, which is impressive and hence shows scope for further improvement.

Furthermore, Table 4D provides State level data pertaining to total assigned revenue for panchayats for the period 1992-93 to 1997-98. For Gram Panchayats, data shows that there was no increase in the transfer of assigned revenues for the initial four years and remained static, but in the subsequent years, the per cent increase recorded to more than 16 per cent (Table 3.2). As stated earlier, the increase is due to per cent increase in the share of Gram Panchayats, as also the release of arrears. The total assigned revenue given to Janpad Panchayats shows increasing trend in absolute terms. The per cent increase for the period 1992-93 to 1997-98 is quite

Table 4D : Total Assigned Revenues to Panchayats

(Rs. in thousands)

Level of Panchayat	1992-93	1993-94	1994-95	1995-96	1996-97	1997-98
ZP	7500	7500	7500	7500	59213	59213
JP	99093	127723	135282	135293	145131	181872
GP	24780	24780	24780	24780	28921	83024
Total	131373	160003	167562	168203	233265	324109

Source: Commissioner of Panchayats, Government of M.P.

erratic (Table 3.6). The trend in percent increase for the year 1994-95 and 1995-96 shows abrupt fall, touching the lowest to 0.5 per cent. In the subsequent years, it has regained and gone up marginally. The reason for the increase is due to enhanced per cent share as also the release of arrears. For Zilla Panchayats (Tables 4D & 3.11), the quantum of funds released was static for the initial four years and a sudden boom is recorded in the year 1996-97; the per cent increase in this year is 689. As mentioned above, it is due to release of revenue from new assignment of royalty from mines and minerals. And in the next year, it is maintaining the same.

Now we will examine the performance of assigned revenues in the sample panchayats. Table 3.3 provides data relating to the sample Gram Panchayats and it shows that the release of assigned revenues is erratic and irregular. Two sample Gram Panchayats did not get any amount for one year. The annual average of assigned revenues to the total receipt (Graph 2) for four sample Gram Panchayats show variation to the maximum of 38 per cent and minimum of 16 per cent. The exact contribution of assigned revenues to the total receipt of sample Gram Panchayats (Col.15, Table 3.1) vary from 0.29 per cent to maximum 2.35 per cent. Graph 2 shows the contribution of annual average of assigned revenues in the sample Gram Panchayats, the maximum is 38 per cent and the minimum of 16 per cent. Therefore, assigned revenues do not constitute much in the composition of finances of sample Gram Panchayats. On expenditure side, the contribution of assigned revenues to the total expenditure of sample Gram Panchayats is almost similar (Col.17, Table 3.3). Graph 4 shows the annual average assigned revenue to total expenditure and it varies from 15 per cent to 40 per cent, more or less than what they receive. The per capita income from assigned revenues in the sample Gram Panchayats (Table 3.4) shows a little contribution and it is always less than one rupee. Therefore, the income from this source does not contribute much at the Gram Panchayats.

In the sample Janpad Panchayats (Table 3.7, Col.15), the contribution of assigned revenues to the total income varies from 4 per cent to 27 per cent. A sharp variation is evident as also it shows declining trend. Nevertheless, the contribution was substantial during 1994-95 and 1995-96 period but it has drastically come down. The annual average of this source to annual average of total receipt is 17 and 10 per cent respectively for two Janpad Panchayats. Graph 9 shows that the annual average of assigned revenue to total receipt was more in one sample JP (Dharmjaygarh). On the expenditure side, it maintains similar situation (Graph 11). The per capita income from assigned revenue in the sample Janpads is more than two rupees which cannot be said to be substantial (Table 3.8). The sample Zilla Panchayat did not receive any amount during the period covered for the study so no data pertaining to assigned revenues is shown in Table 3.9. Therefore, no trend is available for the sample Zilla Panchayat so far assigned revenue is concerned.

Grants-in-aid

Another important form of fiscal institutions in a federal set-up is inter-governmental grants to meet the remaining inadequacy in needs of resources of the recipient government, even after getting share in divisible taxes. In fact, panchayats largely depend upon grants for their existence and survival. Though variety of grants exist, such as, statutory, plan, non-plan, adhoc and discretionary, it can broadly be grouped into two categories: (a) conditional (specific purpose) grant, and (b) unconditional (general purpose) grants. The basic purpose of a grant system at a sub-state level is to serve as an instrument to promote territorial equity among rural-urban areas and also to help equalise the standards of basic social services. Thus, grants are designed to help financially such poor local bodies to ensure the standards of services provided by them.

In case of conditional grant, a condition is attached to ensure not only the grant spent for the purpose intended to be, but also a certain standard is to be maintained. In other words, the grantor defines the purpose for which the recipient is to utilise that fund. The quantum of a specific purpose grant may be determined in various ways. A certain percentage of locally financed expenditure may be assigned to a given service, or, alternatively, a certain amount may be assigned to each unit of need. In contrast to this, the general purpose grants (unconditional), as no such conditions are laid down, the recipient government can utilise this grant as per their own set of priorities.

The conditional grants (specific purpose) have several possible forms. One popular form is matching grant in which, according to a specified formula, the recipient is required to match each grant rupee it accepts with a certain amount of funds from own revenues.

Apart from these two broad categories of grants, there are other types of grants, namely, block grants, establishment grants, road maintenance grants, minor irrigation grants and miscellaneous grants. Majority of these grants are in vogue in many States given to local bodies. A major proportion of total grants given to panchayats is block grants for execution of public works programme based on requirements of these bodies. The allocation of grant depends upon the project proposed by the panchayats therefore quantum of grants vary. This results into building up political influence to attract block grant from the government and hence weak panchayats suffer on this score. The system of giving per capita grant is also unsatisfactory. In this system, grant once fixed remains unchanged for number of years and it is not responsive to changes in the price level or revenue receipt of the State government. It is therefore essential to make grant elastic to match increasing financial requirements of panchayats over time.

Article 243-I (a) (iii) requires the State Finance Commission to make recommendations as to the principles which should govern the grants-in-aid to the panchayats from the Consolidated Fund of the State. In this respect, the task of the SFC is more complex than the Central Finance Commission because various Central Finance Commissions have already laid down guidelines for the allotment of grants to States. Moreover, they have to deal with only one level of government whereas the SFC has to recommend for three layers of panchayats. It may be difficult for the SFC to estimate expenditures and revenues on a normative basis because it has to cover large number of units and, particularly the availability of required data from such huge number of bodies, and to evolve a satisfactory methodology for the purpose.

A rational grant system, though difficult to realise, may form two important considerations: (a) to devise a relevant classification and administration of grants simple and transparent, end (b) to evolve a formula-based grant allocation system (Oommen, 1995). A formula-based allocation of grants and shared taxes may therefore be helpful to serve on a levelling up force to promote regional balanced development and territorial equity within the State. Development grants particularly should be given on the basis of a formula for expanding the services by panchayats. Population could be one important criterion. In addition to this, other criteria, that reflect the need for expansion of services for which grants are given, should also be given appropriate weightage.

As stated above, grants constitute the single largest source of revenue of panchayats in the country. The panchayats in the State of Madhya Pradesh is not exception to this fact.

Grants, therefore, are the major source of revenue for panchayats that is determined by the State government from time to time to carry out assigned functions. Section 64 of the MPPA, 1993 provides that the 'State government shall make grants-in-aid to the panchayats as may be decided on the basis of recommendations of the State Finance Commission.' The State government has prescribed the staff structure of each tier of panchayat as also the honorarium payable to elected functionaries. Accordingly, to meet the expenditure on this, the State government releases grants to them. Tables 3.1, 3.5 and 3.10 provide the nature and quantum of grants given to Gram Panchayat, Janpad Panchayat and Zilla Panchayat respectively.

Table 4E : Total Grants to Panchayats

Panchayat Level	1992-93	1993-94	1994-95	1995-96	1996-97	1997-98
ZP	32477	33343	34956	245181	1161066	1855830
	(0.61)	(0.61)	(0.63)	(4.45)	(20.21)	(31.58)
JP	—	—	—	51381	54380	298082
				(0.93)	(0.97)	(5.25)
GP	292422	382877	377008	527039	720484	2415427
	(8.39)	(10.98)	(10.81)	(15.11)	(20.66)	(69.27)
Total	324899	416220	411964	823601	1935930	4569339

Note : Figures in parenthesis are per capita in Rupees.
Source: Commissioner of Panchayats, Government of M.P.

As discussed earlier, Panchayats in the State get broadly three types of grants, they are: General Purpose Grant, Specific Purpose Grant, Development Purpose Grants. Besides, they also receive grants out of centrally sponsored schemes/ State share in those schemes, Tenth Finance Commission Grants and SFC grants. As per the recommendations of the SFC, Zilla Panchayats are given general purpose grant to meet the administrative and establishment cost. Specific purpose grant is meant for payment of honorarium of elected representatives and for their expenses on training (Table 4.4). Earlier, from 1992-93 to 1994-95, the Department of Panchayat and Social Welfare was releasing the development purpose

Table 4.2 : Devolution of Assigned Revenues to Janpad Panchayats

Year	Items	Total Amount (Lakhs)	Share of Rural Local Bodies	Share of Janpad Panchayats
1990-91	Land Revenue	750.00	50%	10%
	Cess on L.R.	38.00	100%	40%
	Addl. Stamp duty	692.00	100%	100%
	Total	1480.00		
1991-92	Land Revenue	750.00	50%	10%
	Cess on L.R.	38.00	100%	40%
	Addl. Stamp duty	806.47	100%	100%
	Total	1594.47		
1992-93	Land Revenue	750.00	50%	10%
	Cess on L.R.	38.00	100%	40%
	Addl. Samp duty	900.73	100%	100%
	Total	1688.73		
1993-94	Land Revenue	750.00	50%	10%
	Cess on L.R.	38.00	100%	40%
	Addl. Samp duty	1107.03	100%	100%
	Total	1895.03		
1994-95	Land Revenue	750.00	50%	10%
	Cess on L.R.	38.00	100%	40%
	Addl. Samp duty	1262.62	100%	100%
	Total	2050.62		
1995-96	Land Revenue	750.00	50%	
	Cess on L.R.	38.00	100%	
	Addl. Samp duty	1262.62	100%	100%
	Total	2050.62		
1996-97	Land Revenue		100%	
	Cess on L.R.		50%	
	Addl. Samp duty	1444.26	100%	100%
	Additional Cess on Land Revenue by Z.Ps		100%	25%
	Total	1444.26		
1997-98	Land Revenue		50%	
	Cess on L.R.		100%	100%
	Addl. Samp duty	1810.97	100%	25%
	Additonal Cess on Land Revenue by Z.Ps		100%	
	Total	1810.97		
1998-99	Land Revenue	750.00	100%	
	Cess on L.R.	38.00	100%	
	Addl. Samp duty	1107.03	100%	25%
	Additional Cess on Land Revenue by ZPs	1895.03		
	Total	3790.06		

Source : Commissioner of Panchayats, Government of Madhya Pradesh.

Table 4.3 : Devolution of Assigned Revenues to Gram Panchayats

Year	Items	Total Amount (Lakhs)	Share of Rural Local Bodies	Share of Village Panchayats
1990-91	Land Revenue	750.00	50%	30%
	Cess on L.R.	38.00	100%	60%
1991-92	Land Revenue	750.00	50%	30%
	Cess on L.R.	38.00	100%	60%
1992-93	Land Revenue	750.00	50%	30%
	Cess on L.R.	38.00	100%	60%
1993-94	Land Revenue	750.00	50%	30%
	Cess on L.R.	38.00	100%	60%
1994-95	Land Revenue	750.00	50%	30%
	Cess on L.R.	38.00	100%	60%
1995-96	Land Revenue	750.00	100%	100%
	Cess on L.R.	38.00	100%	100%
1996-97	Land Revenue	750.00	100%	100%
	Cess on L.R.	38.00	100%	100%
1997-98	Land Revenue	750.00	100%	100%
	Cess on L.R.	38.00	100%	100%
1998-99	Land Revenue	750.00	100%	100%
	Cess on L.R.	38.00	100%	100%
	Additional Cess on Land Revenue by Zilla Panchayat		100%	50%
	Share of Surcharge on Commercial Tax	194000.00	100%	100%

Source : Commissioner of Panchayats, Government of Madhya Pradesh.

grants to Zilla Panchayats. Subsequently, on the basis of recommendations of the SFC, the concerned departments are releasing funds whose programmes are being implemented by Panchayats. In case of Janpad and Gram Panchayats, the development purpose grant was received only during 1997-98 (Tables 3.5 & 3.1).

Table 4.4 : Devolution of Grants to Zilla Panchayats

Year	Items	Total Amount (Lakhs)	Share of Rural Local Bodies	Share of Zilla Panchayats
1990-91	Grant for conference	3.24	100%	100%
1991-92	Grant for conference	3.24	100%	100%
1992-93	Grant for conference	3.24	100%	100%
1993-94	Grant for conference	8.24	100%	100%
1994-95	Grant for conference	7.8	100%	100%
1995-96	Grant for conference	13.85	100%	100%
1995-96	Grant for conference	1141.81	100%	11%
1996-97	District Panch conference	49.15	100%	100%
1996-97	Honororium to Office bearers	1208.45	100%	11%
	General Purpose Grant	135.67	100%	100%
	Tenth Finance Commission	8717	100%	3%
1997-98	District Panch conference	49.1	100%	100%
1998-99	Honorarium to Office bearers	1235	100%	11%
	General Purpose Grant	150	100%	100%
	Tenth Finance Commission	8717	100%	3%

Source : Commissioner of Panchayats, Government of Madhya Pradesh.

Earlier, the Zilla Panchayats were not the recipient of general purpose grants till the SFC has recommended in 1996. As the SFC recommendations have been accepted by the State government, they are getting general purpose grants. Accordingly (Table 3.10) during 1996-97, ZPs got Rs.13567 thousands in 1997-98 and Rs.15000 thousands next year as general purpose grant to meet their establishment expenditure and it will continue till year 2001. The per capita general purpose grants for these two years comes to 23 paisa and 25 paisa, which is quite inadequate. Janpad Panchayats are not the recipient of this grant even after the SFC recommendations. This is in view of the fact that Janpad Panchayats are getting the additional stamp duty to meet their establishment expenditure. In case of Gram Panchayats

(Table 3.1), general purpose grant is given to meet expenditure on account of salary and allowances of Panchayat Secretaries from 1992-93 and subsequently from 1993-94 for the payment of honorarium of Panchayat Karmis. The honorarium paid to the Gram Panchayats elected functionaries come under general purpose grant whereas, for Janpad and Zilla Panchayats, it is separately given under special purpose grant every year from 1994-95 onwards. Special purpose grants are given to Zilla Panchayats (Table 4.4) and Janpad Panchayats (Table 4.5), which includes honorarium, travelling and other allowances of elected representatives, and for organising training programme for all non-official functionaries of three tiers. The scheme of payment of honorarium and perks to elected representatives was started from 1994-95 onwards, and the government prescribes the amount payable to them. On the basis of the recommendations of the SFC, Gram Panchayats are getting special purpose grants to carry out their specified basic functions for the period 1996-2000. For this purpose, Rs.167.31 crore was released for the first time in 1997-98 to the Gram Panchayats.

Table 4.5 : Devolution of Grants to Janpad Panchayats

Year	Items	Total Amount (Lakhs)	Share of Rural Local Bodies	Share of Janpad Panchayats
1995-96	Honorarium to office bearers	1141.86	100%	45%
1996-97	Honorarium to office bearers	1208.45	100%	45%
	Tenth Finance Commission (TFC)	8717	100%	8%
1997-98	TFC (J.P. Bhawan)	8717	100%	8%
	Honorarium to office bearers	1235	100%	45%
1998-99	TFC (J.P. Bhawan)	8717	100%	8%
	Honorarium to office bearers	1235	100%	45%

Source : Commissioner of Panchayats, Government of Madhya Pradesh.

Before 1994-95, non-official functionaries of Zilla Panchayats were not paid any honorarium, etc., except they were entitled to receive some expenses towards attending meetings, etc., but from this year onwards they are being paid prescribed honorarium, etc. The President to Zilla Panchayat enjoys the rank of minister of State. The prescribed rates of honorarium, etc., are given in the Statement 1.7. It is evident from the Statement 1.7 that at Gram Panchayat level, the honorarium is quite low in proportion to honorarium given to other two higher tiers. Table 4.6 shows that honorarium paid to Panchayat Karmis is more than that of the office bearers.

Another type of grant given to panchayats in the State is development purpose grants. Before the 73rd Amendment,

Table 4.6 : Devolution of Grants to Gram Panchayats

Year	Items	Total Amount (Lakhs)	Share of Rural Local Bodies	Share of Village Panchayats
1995-96	Honorarium to Panchayat Karmi	529.00	100%	100%
	Honorarium to office bearers	1141.81	100%	45%
1996-97	Honorarium to Panchayat Karmi	1360.00	100%	100%
	Honorarium to office bearers	1141.81	100%	45%
	Tenth Finance Commission	8717.00	100%	89%
1997-98	Honorarium to Panchayat Karmi	1360.00	100%	100%
	Honorarium to office bearers	1141.81	100%	45%
	Basic Function of Gram Panchayat (State Finance Commission)	16730.50	100%	100%
	Tenth Finance Commission	8717.00	100%	89%
1998-99	Honorarium to Panchayat Karmi	1360.00	100%	100%
	Honorarium to office bearers	1235.00	100%	100%
	Basic Function of Gram Panchayat (State Finance Commission)	18911.00	100%	100%
	Tenth Finance Commission	8717.00	100%	89%

Source : Commissioner of Panchayats, Government of Madhya Pradesh.

the Panchayat Department was releasing this grant to Zilla Panchayats for the maintenance of hand pumps and water supply system during 1992-93 to 1994-95. Now, this grant has also been extended to Janpad Panchayats from 1997-98. As stated above, funds are being released to panchayats by the concerned departments whose schemes are being implemented by them. In the new arrangement, from 1996-97, the development departments like PHE, Education, Health, Minor Irrigation, Animal Husbandry, Forest, Fisheries, etc., are allocating funds to panchayats in their respective department budget under demand No. 80, 82 and 84. The budgetary allocation of these departments is put under demand No.80 and placed at their disposal.

The grants from the tribal sub-plan and the special component plan are shown in the budget demand No. 82 and 84 respectively. Earlier, before 1996, the budgetary allocation for panchayats was shown in the State budget as demand Nos. 30, 41 and 64. This change has taken place on the basis of the recommendation of SFC. The budgets of these departments show allocation for panchayat sector programmes as grant-in-aid (development grant).

Table 3.10 exhibits a quantum jump in development grant for Zilla Panchayats. It is striking to note that during 1992-93 to 1994-95 the quantum of development grant to ZPs was static to Rs.3 crore annually, which has gone up by seven times to Rupees 21.23 crores in 1995-96. In the subsequent years, it has tremendously jumped to Rupees 111.48 crores in 1996-97 and Rupees 180.96 crores in 1997-98. Thus, the amount of development grants to ZPs shows a steep increasing trend. The per capita development grant for Zilla Panchayats has increased from 54 paisa to Rs. 30.58, which is a substantial growth but low in terms of development purposes. This is due to devolution of more functions. Apart from more functional assignment, their services are also being utilised by the government. The specific purpose grants also show increasing trend but not to the extent of development grant. The total grants to ZPs (Table 4E) have significantly gone up from 1996-97 onwards and the per capita has reached to Rs.31.58. The per cent increase of the total grants given to ZPs (Table 3.11) has increased maximum to 601 per cent in 1995-96 from the lowest of 2.7 per cent in 1993-94. The contribution of grants (excluding TFC grants) to the total receipts of the ZPs in the State was considerably high to the extent of 74 per cent in 1992-93 but it has come down to 24 per cent in 1997-98, though in terms of absolute figures it has gone up enormously. If the TFC grants are also included then it constitutes about 96 per cent. In fact, the quantum of funds released to ZPs under TFC grants are not exclusively for them, rather it is further re-distributed to lower tiers of panchayats. Therefore, this figure cannot be taken as real for the purpose of calculation.

Janpad Panchayats are getting specific purpose grants from 1995-96, and development grant from 1997-98 (Table 3.5). The per capita total grants to JPs have increased from 93 paisa to Rs.5.25. Remarkably, the JPs are not getting as much grants as other two tiers.

As mentioned above and seen in Table 3.1, the Gram Panchayats are getting general purpose grants all through and it shows increasing trend. This is due to increase in the salary of staff and increase in number of employees. To carry out basic functions, they have received Rs.167.31 crores for the year 1997-98. The per capita of this grant is Rs.47.98, which is quite moderate in view of the fact that they have to render various basic services. The SFC has suggested the criteria for this grant. In the next chapter, detail discussion has been provided.

Tables 3.3, 3.7 and 3.9 show the quantum of grants received by the sample Gram Panchayats, Janpad Panchayats and Zilla Panchayats respectively. It is evident from Table 3.3 that there is increase in the grants for all the sample Gram Panchayats, particularly from the period when devolution of functions and the recommendations of SFC has been operationalised. In the sample Gram Panchayats, the per capita grant shows minimum Rs.39 with maximum of Rs.264 (Table 3.4). In all the four sample Gram Panchayats, the trend in per capita grant is on the path of increase, and especially one Gram Panchayat (Kankabira) has registered a quantum jump from Rs.48 to Rs.264. Besides, it also shows that the in total receipts of the sample Gram Panchayats, grants constitute a substantial proportion (Table 3.3). Thus, dependency on grants is quite high. In case of two samples Janpad Panchayats, the per capita grant shows increasing trend from Rs.3 to Rs.114. In sample Janpad Panchayats (Table 3.7, Graph-10), the contribution of grants in the total receipt is quite high. In one sample Janpad (Sarangarh), in year 1997-98, the percentage of grants to total receipt is 99 per cent and the per capita is Rs.114. As pointed out above, Zilla Panchayats mainly depend upon grants, this situation is evident in the sample Zilla Panchayat and it is only grand regime. Table 3.9 shows increase in the amount received as grant in the sample Zilla Panchayats during five-year period.

If assigned revenues and grants put together, the annual average in sample Gram Panchayats, it constitutes major share in the total receipt (Col.16, Table 3.3); its contribution is minimum 87 per cent and maximum 93 per cent. On the expenditure side, it is more than the receipt (Col.18, Table 3.3). Similarly, in the sample Janpad Panchayats, the contribution of both items is quite high and expenditure is higher than it (Table 3.7, Cols.17, 20). The annual average of both items to the total receipts is about half mark and expenditure is almost same (Graphs 13, 14).

So far the financial powers are concerned, panchayats have been vested with power to accord administrative and financial approvals in respect of works entrusted to them under various programmes. Gram Panchayats upto Rs.3 lakh, Janpad Panchayats upto Rs.7 lakh and Zilla Panchayats upto Rs.10 lakh can sanction a work.

Tenth Finance Commission Grants

The Tenth Finance Commission (TFC) has awarded a total sum of Rs.348.68 crore to the state, which is to be given to panchayats during 1999-2000. By now, the State has received two instalments of Rs.871700 thousand in the year 1996-97 and 1997-98. Table 4.7 provides the total amounts received under the TFC and, in turn, funds released by the State government to three-tier panchayats in four instalments. The criteria adopted for *inter se* distribution among panchayats was on (a) rural population, and (b) need based. Accordingly, allocation was made to each tier and fund was released. The government has issued a detail guidelines (1997) for the utilisation of TFC funds by panchayats. The guideline has

Table 4.7 : Tenth Finance Commission Grant

Year	Amount (Rs. in Thousands)
1996-97	871700
1997-98	871700

Tenth Finance Commission Grants Released to Panchayats

Year	Amount Released			Total
	Zilla Panchayats	Janpad Panchayats	Village Panchayats	
1996-97	30000	73500	768200	871700
1997-98	34000	74500	763200	871700

Instalments of Amount Released to Panchayats

Date	Year	Amount Released			Total
		Zilla Panchayat	Janpad Panchayat	Village Panchayat	
20-8-97	1996-97	25600	59200	345200	430000
17-12-97	1996-97	4400	14300	423000	441700
1-9-98	1997-98	29200	73900	496900	60000
1-9-98	1997-98	4800	600	266300	271700
Total		64000	148000	1531400	1203400

Note : Criteria for vertical and horizontal distribution of amounts amongst the different tiers of Panchayats was on (i) Rural Population, (ii) Need based.

Source : Commissioner of Panchayats, Government of Madhya Pradesh.

identified some of the infrastructure development work and a standard specification for some items have been given (Table 4F). While identifying development works under TFC funds, Gram Panchayats will give priority to works like school building, drains, culverts, etc. For the distribution of funds to lower units, a committee has been constituted at the district level under the chairmanship of president of Zilla Panchayat. The selection of works is done at the Janpad level, a special meeting for the purpose is convened under the chairmanship of local MLA, and proposal of works will be discussed and it will approve the works to be taken up in the area. In the selected work, ten per cent matching share is to be paid either by the Gram Panchayat from own sources or from the MLA Local Area Development Fund. As stated above, the guideline contains a list of standardised prescribed works for each tier with unit cost. If these prescribed works are taken up then technical sanction is not required and the

Table 4F : Works to be taken under the Tenth Finance Commission

S.No.	Name of Work	Target	Unit Cost/Work	Total Amt. (Rs. lakhs)
1.	Zilla Panchayat Building			
	(a) Building	25	40.00	1000.00
	(b) Building Extension	20	10.00	200.00
2.	Janpad Panchayat			
	(a) Building	240	10.00	2400.00
	(b) Building Extension	150	2.50	375.00
3.	Gram Panchayat			
	(a) Building	8720	2.00	17440.00
4.	Hingher Sec. School Building	160	7.00	1120.00
5.	High School Building	425	7.00	2975.00
6.	Middle School Building	669	3.00	2007.00
7.	Primary School	750	2.00	1500.00
8.	Sub-Health Centre			
	(a) (10 bed hospital)			
	(b) Sub-health centre	140	4.00	560.00
9.	Kharna/drains/culvert	4507	1.00	4507.00
10.	Drains for hand pump/Water tank for animal	2080	0.15	104.00
11.	Public Platform	12.00	0.15	180.00
	Total			34868.00

cost amount is straightaway released. In course of fieldwork in the sample Gram Panchayats it was mentioned by the sarpanches that in some cases they were not involved while deciding about the works to be taken up in their area. It was more or less decided by the local MLA as the ten per cent share is paid out of MLA funds. Because of the involvement of local MLA in the process of selection of schemes, it was pointed out that some Gram Panchayats could not get any scheme approved for their areas. Thus, all GPs are not recipient of TFC funds.

One sample Gram Panchayat (Sisringa) did not get any fund out of TFC grant. It was also mentioned in one sample Gram Panchayat that the work (public platform) taken up in that village under the TFC scheme has no public utility and it is not being utilised by the villagers. The reasons for these problems are attributed to the dominance of local MLA and political consideration.

In fine, assigned revenues and grants is the major revenue receipt of panchayats in the State. Even then, it appears that the funds available with panchayats is inadequate to meet the local needs and requirements and they are not in a position to provide basic services satisfactorily. Data reveals that there is a remarkable increase in the quantum of grants due to devolution of functions, on the basis of SFC recommendations and TFC funds. It was pointed out that the release of funds to lower tier of panchayats by the higher level body is not timely and hence affects the execution of work.

Loans

One of the sources of finance to panchayat is borrowing and it is an important aspect of local public finance. It is expected that panchayats will tap all source of finance including loans. The Act provides for obtaining loans from State government or financial institutions. The panchayats desirous of taking up any worthwhile project, loans can be raised either from financial institution or open market. The data available do not show any such evidence of borrowings by any panchayat either from the State government or from any financial institution. Among the sample panchayats also, no unit has indicated such loans either. Therefore, obtaining loans by panchayats does not appear to be a common practice. The tendency is more towards getting grants than going for a loan for the development purpose.

5

AN OVERVIEW OF STATE FINANCE COMMISSION

In this chapter, the recommendations of the first Madhya Pradesh State Finance Commission (SFC) and action taken thereon (ATR) by the government has been presented to ascertain the flow of funds to panchayats. To meet the Constitutional obligation under Article 243-I, the State government has constituted the Commission in June, 1994 to make recommendations as mentioned in the terms of reference.

In its first (interim) report in March, 1995, the Commission has recommended that a sum of Rs.130.66 crore be given to Gram Panchayats to carry out basic functions from 1995-96. This amount constitutes 2.91 per cent of the net tax and non-tax revenue of the State. In its final report in June, 1996, the Commission has made several far reaching recommendations covering items given in the terms of reference. While doing so, the Commission reviewed analytically the financial position of State and panchayat bodies in order to reach objective conclusions. The Commission observed that the resources of the State are sinking and commitments are increasing. The available resources of the State has limited scope for further mobilising revenues. In the context of panchayats, the Commission observed that the income of panchayats through own sources is meagre and it is declining regularly in relation to increasing population and they cannot be expected to arrange required funds to implement their own plans and development works. The main source of revenue of panchayats has been from government grants and the quantum of untied grants has been very limited and, as such, it is insufficient to meet even administration expenses.

After analysing various aspects of finances of State and panchayats, the Commission found that the State government has been unable to monitor transfer of due share of taxes to panchayats and committed amount is not being released. Therefore, the Commission found logical to recommend a particular share of gross tax and non-tax revenue of the State instead of shares of specific taxes. Hence, the Commission preferred to adopt the principle of 'global sharing'. While determining the devolution of share, the obligatory functions assigned to village panchayats were taken as a base for calculation. For computing the share, an arithmetic formula was adopted. With regard to inter-district distribution, a formula has been suggested by proper weightage to certain objective criteria and some variables. For inter-panchayat distribution, population and area will be given 75 and 25 per cent weightage respectively.

After having detailed study of budget of some Gram Panchayats regarding sources of revenue and heads of expenditure, the Commission found that the per capita income of these village panchayats are usually 22.44 per cent through their own source, 0.31 per cent through share of taxes from the State government, 46.26 per cent from tied funds for performing various activities, and 30.96 per cent miscellaneous income in the form of loans and advances.

The budget of the State for 1994-95 shows that collection from additional stamp duty was Rs.12 crores, land revenue Rs.7.50 crores and cess on land revenue Rs.38 crores. This has to be distributed to all tiers of panchayats.

Presently, village panchayats are getting an average of Rs.800 only from the budget of the State. This comes to 50 paisa per capita released to Gram Panchayats.

A five year data show that a total sum of Rs. 99.78 crores was collected from land revenue, cess on land revenue and additional stamp duty. As per rules, the government had to release the equivalent amount to panchayat fund, instead only

Rs. 84.96 crores has been provided in the budget for transfer, that is, a sum of Rs.14.82 crores less to be transferred. Despite this provision, only Rs.63.78 crores were paid to panchayats, Rs.36 crores less than the actual revenue. This adversely affects the financial position of rural local bodies. Apart from the short payment, adhocism prevails in determining the inter-district and inter-panchayat distribution of funds.

The recommendations of the Commission and action taken thereon by the government is as follows:

Recommendations	*Response of the Government (ATR)*
1. Share payable to panchayats from the revenues of the State. A sum of Rs.152.33 crore be allocated for 1996-97 to 30922 panchayats from the consolidated fund of the State. The principle of "Global Sharing or Universal Sharing" was recommended for determining the arrears of share of the panchayats from the gross receipts	1. As the report was received in July, 1996, it was, therefore, decided that a share of the total revenue receipts will be allocated from the next financial year. The village panchayats will be allocated 2.91per cent of the gross tax and non-tax revenue receipts for the immediate preceding year during 1997-98. The amount for the year 1997-98 is Rs.167.30 crore.
To compute the share, two alternatives were suggested: (a) 2.19 per cent of tax and non-tax revenues of the State government for the previous year. (b) If the principle of releasing funds from the net revenue	In subsequent decision on 21.03.1997, 2.91 per cent as recommended by the State Finance Commission be disbursed to village panchayats but after deducting proceeds of the land revenue from the tax revenue of the previous year. The State government

Recommendations	*Response of the Government (ATR)*
of the State is adopted, then an amount equal to 3.24 per cent of net proceeds of total revenue of the preceeding year is recommended to be released. While computing the net receipts, the limit of administrative expenditure on collection of revenue would be committed to a maximum of 10 per cent of the gross revenue.	received the Commission's report in July 1996 and accepted its recommendations to allocate and disburse Rs.167.30 crore only from the year 1997-98. The recommendation to allocate Rs.152.33 crore for the year 1996-97 was not accepted.
2. The present practice of allocation by way of Grant-in-aid to the panchayats from the revenue collected in the previous year from land revenue, land revenue cess and additional stamp duty be done away with.	2. The recommendation has been accepted.
3. Formula for inter-district distribution	3. Formula has been accepted.
For determining the percentage share of a district, the SFC devised a formula, giving weightage to every district for its population, area, backwardness and prosperity and left no scope of any ambiguity in distribution of	

Recommendations	*Response of the Government (ATR)*
4. Inter-panchayat distribution weightage in the proportion of 75:25 respectively for population and area for the allocation of funds among panchayats of a district.	4. The Grant received by a district be allocated to the panchayats of the district giving weightage of: 70 per cent for population; 25 per cent for area; and 5 per cent for tax collection. Funds are being released to the panchayats in the districts according to the norms recommended. The Government has issued guidelines called "*Gram Panchayat ke moolbhoot karyon ke liye anudan — Margadarshika*". It contains guidelines for distribution of funds to the panchayat, purpose and utilisation of funds, its audits, etc. The basic functions outlined are : sanitation, conservation, construction and maintenance of public wells for supply of drinking water, village roads, culverts, bridges, latrines, drains, cattle ponds, lighting of village streets, prevention of fire; plantation; management and regulation of markets, shops, eating houses; prevention of contagious diseases, etc. The priorities fixed by the Government for the year 1997-98 are:

Recommendations	*Response of the Government (ATR)*
	(i) Supply of potable water in villages and their hamlets. (ii) Deeping of water tanks, repairs, construction, etc. (iii) Construction and repair of primary and middle school buildings. (iv) Construction of Health Centres/Maternity Homes and equipments. (v) Construction of approach roads connecting main roads. (vi) Construction of drains, *kharanja*. (vii) Construction of Gram Panchayat Bhawan and *Chabutara*. (viii) Construction of water storage near old hand pumps.
5. General Purpose Grant: In keeping with the prevailing practice, Janpad Panchayats and District Panchayats be given General Purpose Grant of Rs.14.65 crore and Rs.1.50 crore respectively for the base year 1995-96 and based on this an annual increase of 10 per cent be made.	5. Rs.1.50 crore will be paid annually to the District Panchayats by way of General Purpose Grant. The recommendation of payment of Rs.14.65 crore to Janpad Panchayats has not been accepted.

Recommendations	*Response of the Government (ATR)*
6. Committed Grant—Specific Purpose Grant: A specific purpose committed grant be given by various departments of the government to the panchayats for work which ought to be executed through them.	6. The Government has accepted this recommendation. Departments like Public Health Engineering (Drinking water supply) place funds for the maintenance and upkeep of hand pumps to the PRIs.
7. General Grant—For delegated programmes: For conducting/running programmes delegated to the Panchayati Raj Institutions, 2.5 per cent of the total provision made for the programmes should be allocated by way of agent grant which may be adjusted by the department concerned in its budget.	7. No agent grant needs to be paid for work entrusted fully for execution to the panchayats. However, for any special work (which panchayats are not authorized to take up on their own) assigned to the panchayats by the State government the panchayats shall be paid agent grants at the rate recommended by the Commission.
8. Incentive Grant A procedure for making incentive grants to the panchayats should be ordered and the State government should lay down targets of revenue recovery for the panchayats. Panchayats exceeding the target should be given incentive grant by way of award.	8. A system of award was already in vogue. The recommendations for making incentive grant to the panchayats have been accepted. One of the indicators will be work done by the panchayat in the sphere of revenue recovery. Even before the 73rd Constitution Amendment, there

Recommendations	*Response of the Government (ATR)*
	was a system of awarding prize to the Gram Panchayats for their outstanding performance in development work as under:
	At the State level : Rs.1.00 lakh
	At Divisional level : Rs.0.50 lakh
	At District level : Rs.0.25 lakh
	At Development Block level: Rs.0.10 lakh
	On the 20th August 1994, the "Adhikar Diwas" to transfer powers to the three tiers Panchayati Raj was celebrated. A new scheme of giving award to all the three tier Panchayati Raj Institutions was declared, as indicated below:
	Best Gram Panchayat : Rs.5 lakh
	Best Janpad Panchayat : Rs.25 lakh

Recommendations	*Response of the Government (ATR)*
	Best Zilla Panchayat : Rs.50 lakh
	In 1996-97 its scope and content were further enlarged and it was decided to reward one Gram Panchayat in every Development Block, Janpad Panchayat in every Revenue division and one Zilla Panchayat in the State for their outstanding performance as follows:
	Best Gram Panchayat in Development Block: Rs.0.25 lakh
	Best Janpad Panchayat in a Revenue Division: Rs.50.00 lakh
	Best Zilla Panchayat in the State : Rs.25.00 lakh
	Consequently the expenditure incurred by the State government on this score was 64.15 lakh in 1996-97 which has increased to Rs.224.75 lakh in 1997-98.
	In the Commission's view the main emphasis on incentive

Recommendations	*Response of the Government (ATR)*
	grant was to encourage local administration for the fuller exploitation of their own resources. The criteria laid down by the State government includes raising revenue through taxes as one of the seven criteria and assigns it 10 out of 100 marks on this score at the Gram Panchayat level and 5 out of 100 marks at the Janpad Panchayat level. Thus, purpose of encouraging the PRIs through incentive grants *i.e.*, to mobilise their own resources does not appear to be fulfilled. The Commission had suggested that private organizations should evaluate the revenue raising capacity and efforts made in that direction by every local body. As reported, the State government has not made such attempt so far.
9. Establishment Grant: The State government has prescribed certain norms for the payment of honorarium and other facilities to the office bearers of the three tier Panchayati Raj Institutions and	9. The government has accepted the recommendation for payment of grant of Rs.67.66 crore for establishment. The State government has laid down the norms for the payment

Recommendations	*Response of the Government (ATR)*
prescribe administrative structures for their establishments. In view of the guidelines issued by the State government, an amount Rs.67.76 crore of committed expenditure should be released in the form of "establishment grant-in-aid", with effect from the base year 1995-96 (in the forthcoming years by assessing actual expenditure).	of honorarium, allowances, etc., for the elected representatives.
Lump sum non-recurring grant	
10. The State government should sanction one time non-recurring grant for furnishing and maintenance of offices of Panchayati Raj Institutions.	10. Government did not accept this recommendation. It was argued that expenditure on furnishing and maintenance of offices should be met from the amounts of taxes transferred to PRIs by the State government, establishment grant and their other resources.
Specific grant-in-aid (Recommendation of 10th Finance Commission).	
11. 50 per cent of the amount received as per recommendation of the 10th Finance Commission *i.e.*,	11. Since the amount recommended by the 10th Finance Commission is to be spent in accordance

Recommendations	*Response of the Government (ATR)*
Rs.43.58 crore should be distributed among Gram Panchayats in the form of "General Purpose Grant" this sum is based on the 1971 census population, at the rate of Rs.12.50 per capita.	with the guidelines issued by the Government of India, State government did not accept this recommendation.
12. Additional Resources (a) Revenue Forests The management and maintenance of revenue forests in the geographical area of the village panchayat should be entrusted to the village panchayats, which could become their reliable and continuous source of revenue. (b) Agricultural Product Market A revenue of about Rs.50 to 60 crores should be raised for panchayats by rationalising the rates of fees through some new Act or by amending Panchayat Adhiniyam.	12. Both these recommendations are still pending with the State government.
13. Establishment of Village Development Fund	13. The State government did not accept this recommendation.

Recommendations

In order to encourage the process of raising additional funds by way of institutional finance, a rural development fund be established out of remaining 50 per cent *i.e.,* Rs.43.58 crore received following the recommendations of the 10th Finance Commission. This amount should be utilised specially for providing guarantee for projects for drinking water supply or by way of margin money. For the management and administration of this fund, the establishment of a separate agency with an authorised capital of about Rs. 5000 crore should be considered.

14. Budget indicators

The State Finance Commission also examined the procedure of keeping separate accounts in respect of expenditure relating to "tribal area sub-plan" and "special area component plan" for scheduled castes for which separate demand numbers 42 and 68 respectively have been assigned by the State government. Till then, the State

Response of the Government (ATR)

14. The budgetary indicators recommended by the Commission have been accepted. Accordingly, flow of the amount to the institutions and overall position of schemes will be shown under grant Nos. 80, 82 and 84.

The State government, for rural local bodies, in their budget for the year 1996-97 has started

Recommendations	*Response of the Government (ATR)*
government in regard to local bodies was following no separate accounting method. In order to introduce transparency in the budgetary system of the State, the SFC recommended to create separate demand for showing flow of following funds from the state budget to local bodies.	the following demand Nos.:
"A" As grant-in-aid	Demand No.80: Financial assistance to three tiers Panchayati Raj Institutions.
This may include grant-in-aid for establishment expenditure and also specific and general purpose grants-in-aid.	Demand No. 82: Financial assistance to three tiers Panchayati Raj Institutions under tribal sub-plan.
"B" As an agent	Demand No. 84: Financial assistance to three tiers Panchayati Raj Institutions under special component plan for scheduled castes.
Provisions for the activities to be transferred to the local bodies from different departments or to be implemented through the local bodies.	
"C" As share of taxes/fees	
Share of taxes/fees to be assigned to the local bodies on the basis of recommendations of State Finance Commission under Article 243-I and 243-Y of the Constitution. The amount	

Recommendations

followed to the panchayat institutions and the overall position of the schemes have been shown under grant Nos. 80, 82 and 84

80 — Share from the resources of the State (Districtwise)

82 — As grant-in-aid

84 — As and agent

15. Districtwise Distribution of the Revenue

The Commission has recommended that a specific portion of the resources of the state (Tax and non-tax revenue) be allocated to the Gram Panchayats and directed that this should be shown districtwise under of sub-head "share from the State" of the newly created heads 80, 82 and 84.

Response of the Government (ATR)

15. As per the recommendations of the Commission, the districtwise distribution of the share payable to the panchayats from the tax and non-tax revenue of the State will be shown under the sub-head "share from the state" under demand Nos. 80, 82 and 84.

From the financial year 1996-97, the concerned departments of the State government are following this recommendation and budgetary allocations are shown accordingly.

16. The State government has

Recommendations	*Response of the Government (ATR)*
16. Performance Budget Every department should prepare a performance budget separately showing the districtwise provision and targets of delegated programmes, and immediately after approval of the budget the department should release the allocated amount to the district under intimation to the panchayat department and monitor the programmes and expenditure.	agreed to the recommendations of the Commission regarding performance budget. Various departments of the government will frame separate performance budgets showing districtwise provisions and targets in accordance with the recommendations of the Commission. To lay down proper procedure for this, the recommendation will be enforced from the financial year 1998-99. Various departments of the State government are following this recommendation from the financial year 1998-99.
17. *Annual Plan* : In the context of the performance budget, the Commission recommended that the three-tier Panchayats in each district will frame annual plan of operation and there should be constantly monitoring of the plan.	17. The recommendation on the framing of annual plan of operation by the three-tier PRIs in the district and their constant monitoring by them has been accepted. Under sub-section (ii) of section 49-A of the Madhya Pradesh Panchayat Raj Adhiniyam, 1998, it has been laid down as a

Recommendations	*Response of the Government (ATR)*
	function of the Gram Panchayat to prepare annual plans for economic development and social justice of panchayat area. It will be submitted to the Janpad Panchayat within the prescribed time for integration with the Janpad Panchayat plan.
	Amendments in sub-section (i) of Section 50 pertaining to the functions of the Janpad Panchayat and in sub-section (i) of Section 52 pertaining to Zilla Panchayat have also been notified.
18. Review of delegated powers: The order of the State government dated 8th August, 1994 relating to the delegation of powers to the panchayats be reviewed to bring them in conformity with the subjects mentioned in Schedule 11 of Article 243-G of the Constitution and to make them more meaningful.	18. The recommendation regarding review of powers delegated to the Panchayats has been accepted. As per this recommendation, the State government has reviewed the delegation of powers issued on the 8th August 1994. Accordingly, the State government has issued instructions in detail in regard to the functions and responsibilities. This has been compiled in a booklet called "*Paripatron ke sankalan*" in Hindi.

Recommendations	*Response of the Government (ATR)*
	Subsequently, Chief Secretary dated 3rd August 1998, like the one issued in 1994, issued another booklet with a foreword.

Release of Funds

As a follow-up of the recommendations and action taken thereon, the Government has released funds to panchayats. Funds were not made available to panchayats during 1996-97 because the report was submitted late. The following funds were released to panchayats for the year 1997-98.

(i) Rs. 167.30 crore were given to village panchayats to perform basic services on the basis of 2.91 per cent of the total tax and non-tax revenue of the state. It was disbursed in three instalments.

First Instalment — Rs. 42 crore (25% of the total), August 7, 1997
Second Instalment — Rs. 64 crore, August 7, 1997
Third Instalment — Rs. 167.30 crore, March 7, 1998.

(ii) All the three-tier panchayats got Rs.67.67 crore as establishment grants.
(iii) Rs. 1.50 crore to Zilla Panchayats as untied grant.
(iv) Rs. 14.4 crore to Janpad Panchayats out of additional stamp duty as general purpose grant.
(v) Rs. 7 crore and Rs.3.50 crore will be paid locally to Gram Panchayats out of land revenue and cess on land revenue respectively.
(vi) Rs. 87.17 crore released to all three-tier panchayats out of Tenth Finance Commission award for the development of basic infrastructure.

Release for the Year 1998-99

For basic services, on the basis of 2.91 per cent of the total tax and non-tax revenue of the State, the amount comes to Rs. 18911 lakh. This has been released in two instalments.

First Instalment — Rs.4724.75 lakh, *vide* dated 28-7-98.
Second Instalment — Rs.4727.25 lakh, *vide* dated 27-11-98

Above funds were released on the basis of prescribed norms of the Commission to panchayat under various categories of allocation.

Critical Analysis

Indeed, the tasks of thc SFC are very onerous and challenging as compared to the Central Finance Commission due to variety of limitations and difficulties. Nevertheless, the report deserves compliments and provides a new ground for future Commissions. A good attempt has been made to maintain the spirit of the Constitution to strengthen the financial base of PRIs according to their entitlement in view of the general deterioration in the finances of the State.

An alternative approach adopted by the Commission to determine a definite quantum of funds payable to Gram Panchayats for performing obligatory functions is practical and apt. These basic services are local in nature, based on local needs it should be performed only by the local unit, not by the higher unit of administration. Due to proximity, Gram Panchayat is the suitable institutional vehicle to render basic services. If the Gram Panchayats can perform these obligatory functions satisfactorily, its credibility as the grass-roots local institution will enhance and the delivery of services will considerably increase. Hitherto these services are not up to mark due to insufficient resources. Now, the flow of fund will be regular and continuous and hence there will be improvement in the quality of basic services.

The principle of sharing of resources from the gross revenue (tax and non-tax) of the State has distinct advantages and will benefit the local bodies immensely in fiscal devolution. The Tenth Finance Commission has also suggested the principle of pooling of total tax revenue for the purpose of determining devolution. This principle holds strong ground from the system of sharing revenues from only a few specified taxes. This will facilitate the resource flows more predictable, clear and transparent. As it is easy to determine the quantum of gross tax and non-tax revenue of the State, the discrepancies and inconsistencies in calculating the proportion of divisible taxes can be overcome. Further, the Panchayati Raj Institutions will automatically get share in the aggregate buoyancy in revenue collection of the State. Moreover, it will curb the indecision of the government in the determination of rate of particular taxes, which are usually kept pending for long time, and tendency of reducing the tax-rate on their own. Thus, the State-local government fiscal transfer will be rational with positive direction. The choice is more logical and relevant in view of the existing devolution pattern in the State. This recommendation has since been accepted by the government, it is indicative of the fact that the State government will also be in a comfortable position in sharing of resources with the local bodies.

Another remarkable point is the inclusion of the non-tax revenue in the scheme of sharing of resources. It will widen the scope of devolution and local bodies will get more shares in the cake. As indicated, the existing transfer by the State to local bodies is 0.061 per cent whereas by the new formula it will go up by 53 times more.

An equitable formula suggested for the *inter se* distribution among different panchayats will systematise and curb adhocism in the existing system of distribution of funds. The indicators suggested will take care of regional disparities and variations and bring equity and social justice. The formula will enable the needy and backward areas to get more allocation of funds. The prosperity indicator has been given negative weightage by using distance method in the allocation criteria so that the less-developed districts will get proportionately higher allocation of funds than developed districts.

The *inter se* distribution of funds among village panchayats within a district, weightage has been given only to population and area indicators. But, while accepting the formula for distribution of funds to village panchayats, the government has included 5 per cent weightage to tax collection and population criteria has been reduced by 5 per cent. The weightage given to tax collection effort by village panchayats is essential in view of the fact that there is a general reluctance on the part of local leaders to mobilise resources. It will activate local leaders in the endeavour of revenue collection, which is neglected and avoided due to variety of reasons. Consequently, it will improve the performance of village panchayats in resources mobilisation efforts and a sense of competitiveness among panchayats will emerge.

With regard to the grants to these bodies, the Commission has gone beyond the existing system of grants, which is not based on scientific, equitable and systematic norms. Therefore, the Commission evolved its own principles for grants. It is based on the principle of horizontal equity so that variations in the financial needs and taxable capacity of local bodies can be taken care, proper utilisation of funds, sound financial management system, dispensing with the system of adhocism, transparency in distribution of grants, etc. The scheme of grants will help panchayats to estimate in advance the quantum of funds likely to come and accordingly they can plan for the best use of funds. It will facilitate to develop sound financial base thereby minimum level of services can be maintained and priorities can be easily determined.

Among the various grants suggested by the Commission, the general purpose grants will be given to Janpad and District Panchayat. An amount of Rs.16.15 crore calculated on the basis of prevailing practice as the base, the Commission recommended the release of the amount with ten per cent annual increase. The annual increase of ten per cent will take care of inflation and increase in expenditure of these bodies. According to Action Taken Report, the government did not accept the recommendation of the Commission but, surprisingly, it has been released to Janpads also.

The ideals of the Commission to de-link Janpad and District Panchayats from global sharing principle, as suggested for Village Panchayats, is a lopsided view. The promise that these two higher level of bodies do not enjoy autonomy in view of fact that they do not have taxation powers and delegation of tasks are minimal, do not sound logical and appropriate. Truly speaking, the power to impose tax is undoubtedly one of the attributes of local government but it does not mean that in the absence of such power they loose their status of local government. Similarly, devolution of powers to these bodies, by and large, depend upon the State government despite the Constitutional provision of Article 243G and Eleventh Schedule. As a result, these two higher layers of panchayats can be treated as agent of government. The basis is fallacious and it is preposterous to the letter and spirit of the Constitution. All the three layers of panchayats should be considered as a composite whole and they cannot be separated for different purposes. Also, the district level body is considered as suitable unit of administration at the cutting edge level, a fulcrum of administrative system, and it has to guide and direct lower level units. Such proposition will dilute and cut the idea of strengthening the district level body and hence the basic objective of the 73rd Constitution Amendment will be defeated. Similarly, the power to impose tax and collection is given only to village panchayat because of locational convenience and its proximity. This does not entail that the higher level bodies should be treated as agent. This view of the Commission, however, needs to be reconsidered so that it should not give wrong signals and create further confusions in the process of strengthening of these bodies. Therefore, it would be appropriate to consider devolution of funds from the proceeds of tax and non-tax revenue of the State to all the tiers of panchayats. The future Commission may like to reconsider this aspect in proper perspective.

Another category of grant suggested by the Commission is tied grant for delegated programmes. This will take care of plan side allocation funds of various departments in their budget. The idea to have a separate demand number in the departmental budget itself will ensure certainty in the devolution of funds from the plan allocation of each department. This again, depends largely upon the scheme of devolution of powers, functions and responsibilities to these bodies. In this connection, the suggestion of the powers to panchayats is worthwhile. This will ensure more consistent and practical sharing of works by the local institutions for which it has been created. The government has also agreed upon this suggestion.

The suggestion to pay 2.5 per cent to panchayats as agent charges for the sponsored programmes. This has been accepted in a modified way by the government. In the State of Maharashtra, the items outside the purview of the transferred subjects to panchayats, if any, work is entrusted to panchayats for execution, agency charge is paid to them. This is paid for the utilisation of services of the local bodies, and in turn, they earn reasonable amount from it, which can be spent, as they like.

The suggestion of the Commission to encourage panchayats by awarding them for the collection of revenue will make panchayats more conscious towards their duty and a sense of competitiveness will prevail. Such incentive grants are already in practice in other States.

To meet various establishment costs of panchayats, the recommendation of establishment grant is essential and practical. In some States, establishment grants or per capita grant is given for the purpose. This will also take care of the future expenditure in view of further delegation of powers and deployment of staff in these bodies. This has been accepted by the government whereas the recommendation of non-recurring one-time grant to these bodies for office maintenance has not been accepted. This one-time grant would have definitely helped the panchayats in view of the fact that several panchayat units do not have proper infrastructure facilities.

To strengthen the financial base of panchayats, the recommendation of the Commission for tapping additional resources is a better suggestion. In this category two items were identified, firstly, revenue from forest and secondly, agricultural product market. These two items are still under the consideration of the government. In fact, if it is accepted it will boost the economy of the local government. In the recent enactment of Parliament, extending panchayats in the Scheduled Areas, the Gram Panchayats have been empowered to collect revenue from the forest. Therefore, the government may ultimately agree upon this suggestion in future.

6

SUMMARY AND MAJOR FINDINGS

Recognising the fact that inadequacy of finances of panchayats has been a major impediment in its effective functioning, the State-local fiscal relations in the wake of the 73rd Constitutional Amendment have gained a new impetus and significance. Considering the emerging new trends in fiscal federalism, the present study sets out with the objective of examining the fiscal transfers between the State and panchayats particularly with reference to assigned revenues and grants. An attempt has also been made to identify the shortcomings in the existing set-up and the plausible remedial measures. Undoubtedly, panchayats are heavily dependent upon exogenous sources. The functional responsibilities must match with the resource transfer. Therefore, a rational flow of funds from higher levels of government is crucial to rational fiscal relations. The nature and magnitude of flow of funds has direct bearing upon the degree of fiscal decentralisation envisaged and being practiced. The financial transfers, however, should be based on normative criteria reflecting the relative fiscal needs.

Keeping in view the recent endeavours to strengthen financial base of panchayats, and examining the State-panchayat fiscal relations, this study was taken up in the State of Madhya Pradesh. The State has distinction of being the first State to enact Panchayat Act in conformity with the mandated provisions of the 73rd Constitutional Amendment and several initiatives have been taken to revitalise and strengthen the system of local governance. Due to several interventions by the State government, panchayat system has undergone significant changes and several strides have been made. Therefore, it was decided to take up this study in Madhy.. Pradesh. For the purpose of data collection, one Zilla Panchayat was selected thereafter two Janpad Panchayats within the selected district was taken up for the study. Further, four Gram Panchayats, two Gram Panchayats within each selected Janpad Panchayat were selected for indepth study.

The new dispensations of Panchayats have made significant strides in respect to functional assignment. The Madhya Pradesh Panchayat Raj Adhiniyam, 1993 (MPPA) provides list of subjects entrusted to them in accordance with the Eleventh Schedule of the Constitution. Section 53 of the MPPA, 1993 states that the State government by general order or specific order may entrust functions to these bodies. Thus the devolution of functions and powers have been left for executive orders. In accordance with the provision, an order of the Chief Secretary has been issued on August 8, 1994 enlisting the programmes and activities of eighteen departments that have been assigned to them. The notification has clear delineation of functional responsibilities based on the principle of divisibility in terms of execution at the district level; avoidance of duplication or overlapping of functions and better delivery of services. Even then, in fact, these institutions and its elected functionaries do not enjoy such powers and authority, as it should be. The government order merely involves panchayats in implementation, maintenance, supervision, control, inspection and compliance of government orders, monitoring and reporting. Surprisingly, the elected functionaries are not well aware with the assignments entrusted to them; therefore, they are not utilising those powers and function to the fuller extent. This calls for essentially to conduct sensitisation programmes for functionaries associated with these bodies. As much as, the required human and financial resources to match with the transfer of powers have not been put under their control. The steps were also taken to strengthen the staff position to carry out assigned functions.

The merger of DRDA with Zilla Panchayat and block administration with Janpad Panchayat is significant administrative decision. The expected results in the administrative functioning of these two levels of bodies are yet to take shape. A clear demarcation between the original staff of these bodies and transferred staff is visible in terms of their service conditions, benefits, etc. The proper assimilation and operationalisation of two different sets of bodies are yet to take place. It is, therefore, necessary to sort out anomaly in service conditions. Also, steps should be taken to amalgamate the functional responsibilities of two sets of functionaries.

The structure of fiscal composition comprises tax revenues, non-tax revenues, assigned revenues, grants and loans. In the sphere of own sources, taxes, fees and non-tax revenues are the main sources. Gram Panchayats are empowered to impose taxes as specified in the Act, as also Janpad Panchayats are given some taxable items, but Zilla Panchayats are not vested with any taxation powers. At the Gram Panchayat level, the contribution of tax revenue is not significant, as it is maximum 2.99 per cent to the total receipts and the per capita income from tax is about one rupee. Among the taxes, contribution of water tax is more and shows increasing trend. The per cent increase in tax shows increasing trend. Thus, the tax revenue has scope and potential to mobilise further provided local leaders take initiative and come out of rhetorical reasons for non-compliance of tax collection. Profession tax could be a good source if it is tapped. Besides, among the new avenues, Mandi tax would be considered for new tax assignment, as it has potential and scope in rural areas of the State. Gram Panchayats are not even imposing obligatory taxes indicated in the Act. Some punitive action should be thought of for such Gram Panchayats.

The Janpad Panchayat has mainly two tax items to levy, *i.e.*, entertainment tax and development tax. The income out of these sources is not encouraging. Some of the measures suggested in this report that would be the plausible answer to mobilise internal resources and to improve the tax administration.

The non-tax sources of revenue appear to have better scope if it is exploited properly and objectively. All the three layers of panchayat could augment more income from non-tax sources. Data pertaining to non-tax revenue to panchayats shows increasing trend and its contribution to total receipts is higher than tax revenue. Some of the sources of non-tax revenue like auction of ferry ghats and leasing out of fisheries ponds have better scope if it is objectively exploited.

The expenditure of these bodies has also increased in view of increase in the staff strength and transfer of functions. At Gram Panchayat, the expenditure on administration is more than expenditure on services. It shows that services rendered are not up to the expectation and funds available for services are less. Though Gram Panchayats are supposed to provide atleast basic services to the rural people and for which funds are being devolved on the recommendation of the SFC. The expenditure on development grants is quite high which would lead to capital formation. At other two higher tiers, the expenditure pattern shows more expenditure on administration and development than service sector. As their own income is quite less, they are not concentrating on providing services. Therefore, emphasis should be given on mobilisation of own resources and providing quality services.

The focus of the study is on financial devolution; an attempt has been made to examine inter-governmental fiscal transfers. The mode of fiscal transfer is usually in the form of assigned revenues and grants. Two important State taxes (land revenue, cess on land revenue and additional stamp duty) are shared with the panchayats. In the new arrangement, only Gram Panchayats get proceeds of land revenue and cess on land revenue after deducting the collection charges by the revenue department. Janpad Panchayat gets share in additional stamp duty. The other assigned revenue is the share of royalty from the exploitation of Minor Minerals to Panchayat from

1997. It has been observed that the funds in accordance with the due share are not released to panchayats on time. The SFC has also found similar situation.

Apart from these two tiers of Panchayat, Zilla Panchayat has been empowered to raise cess on land revenue upto ten times, *i.e.*, upto ten rupees for each rupee of land revenue. But so far no Zilla Panchayat has exercised this power and hence they could not mobilise additional resources available with them. This needs special attention to pursue them to exercise this power to raise income level.

Among the assigned revenues, additional stamp duty is the major sources of fund, which is transferred to Janpad Panchayats only. The per cent share of additional stamp duty to total assigned revenues ranges between 56 to 75 per cent. The share of release of funds from additional stamp duty in absolute terms show increasing trend and the per capita revenue has also increasing trend (maximum Rs.3.20 in 1997-98). The release of funds on this account is not timely and full share is not paid every year. Therefore, steps should be taken for timely release of full share.

Another assigned revenue is share from land revenue and cess thereon. Significantly, the land revenue share has been doubled in five-year period from Rs. 3.75 crore in 1992-93 to Rs.7.50 crore, whereas cess on land revenue remained almost constant. The royalty from Minor Minerals has also increased though it was started from 1997. The assignment of minor minerals is not fully utilised by panchayats; therefore, they are not getting expected income out of it. The overall performance in terms of share of assigned revenues has increasing trend and it has gone up by more than double.

The per capita assigned revenue shows quantum jump from Rs.2.91 in 1992-93 to Rs.6.58 in 1997-98 for all the three tiers put together. In case of Zilla Panchayat, the per capita revenues have increased from 14 paisa to Rs.1.02 during this period, which is not substantial. As compared to this, the per capta of Gram Panchayat has gone up tremendously from 72 paisa to Rs.3.38. This is due to increase in the share of land revenue on the basis of recommendation of SFC, as they are made responsible for providing basic services to people. Among the assigned revenues, the share of additional stamp duty in terms of per capita has gone up about three-folds whereas other items did not go up in the similar manner.

Another important form of fiscal transfer is grants. Generally, grants constitute the single largest source of revenue to panchayats across the country. The panchayats of Madhya Pradesh are not exception to this. The types of grants given to panchayats are establishment grants to all the three-tiers to meet salary of staff as per prescribed staffing pattern; grants to meet payment of honorarium to office bearers; general purpose grants to Zilla Panchayat to meet office expenditure; grant for basic functions of Gram Panchayat on the basis of recommendations of SFC; and Tenth Finance Commission grants. Apart from this, assigned revenues are also given to panchayats in the shape of grants like additional stamp duty and commercial tax grant, but in this study we have classified them into the assigned revenues to avoid confusion. Moreover, panchayats get development grants from the concerned departments whose programmes are entrusted to them.

Zilla Panchayat is getting General Purpose grants on the basis of recommendations of the SFC from 1996 and the per capita of this grant is 23 paisa, which is inadequate. Janpad Panchayats do not get such grant rather they meet their establishment expenditure out of funds released from additional stamp duty. Gram Panchayats do get General Purpose grant to meet expenses for payment of salary and allowances of Panchayat Secretary and Panchayat Karmi. The per capita General Purpose grant for Gram Panchayat has gone up from Rs.8 to Rs.21. It is due to large number of Panchayat Karmi deployed at Gram Panchayats in the State. Gram Panchayat also gets specific purpose grant for basic functions from 1997 and its per capita is Rs.47.

Zilla Panchayat gets development grant and it has substantially increased after 1996 and the per capita development grant has jumped from 56 paisa in 1992-93 to Rs.30 in 1997-98. Janpad Panchayat is getting this grant from 1995 onwards. Gram Panchayats do not get such grant. Panchayats are also getting TFC grants and for which the government has prescribed guidelines. However, all Gram Panchayats are not getting TFC fund as the MLAs have say in allocating the work under the scheme. Therefore, some Gram Panchayats are deprived of getting TFC funds. It is expected that TFC grants should be distributed to all units on normative criteria and it should be untied fund so that each unit can plan to spend this fund to meet local requirements.

It is abundantly clear that the financial base of Panchayats has improved to some extent due to flow of funds from higher level of government, especially after the implementation of SFC recommendations and devolution of more functions to them. Remarkably, data reveals a clear demarcation and high flow of funds to panchayats before and after the Action Taken Report of the State government on the recommendation of SFC. The release of grant is not timely and consequently it hampers work. Whatever may be the quantum jump in funding from grants, the fact remains that it is inadequate to meet the requirements and aspirations of people.

The last chapter of the study has discussions on the main recommendations of the State Finance Commission, action taken thereon by the government, and subsequent follow-up action. Keeping in view the objectives of the study, it is necessary to provide discussion on the SFC separately because the recommendations have bearing upon State-panchayats fiscal relations in the State. To meet the constitutional requirements, the State Finance Commission was constituted in June, 1994 and its final report was submitted in June, 1996. The Commission has given a far reaching recommendations by which flow of funds to panchayat has substantially increased. Among the major recommendations, the Commission has suggested to devolve 2.19 per cent of tax and non-tax revenue of the State, it is to be shared on the principle of 'Global sharing'. This amount will be paid to Gram Panchayats to provide basic services to the people. The Commission has also suggested a formula for *inter se* distribution of funds to make it more rational, to avoid ambiguity and adhocism in distribution of share. The government has accepted majority of its recommendations and funds have been released accordingly. The Commission's recommendations may facilitate in laying the foundations of stronger decentralisation, it will promote regional balance, and it will ensure certain basic services to the people that is expected of them. At last, the report will be a good point of reference to future SFC. Evidently, it has helped strengthening of the financial base of panchayat. The normative criteria suggested by SFC is practical, transparent and will meet the requirements of panchayats. The formula adopted for *inter se* distribution of funds will take care of regional imbalances. While accepting the recommendation of SFC, the State government inclusion of tax effort as criteria for *inter se* distribution is highly logical. This will take care of those panchayats who are inactive in tax collection.

The feasibility of strengthening State-panchayat fiscal relations is the moot question under examination in this study. It can be seen that even in the face of Central Government policy favouring decentralisation and endeavours made by the State government in this regard, the Panchayats fiscal performance did not improve as expected to be. Despite policy declarations, fiscal decentralisation is not taking shape to the extent that panchayats financial system can take place in the context of considerable strength. Though the basic system of Panchayats fundamentally appears to be sound, there are changes that need to be made. This calls for better workable system in administrative procedure, financial autonomy and devolution of function alongwith functionaries and funds. Furthermore, the spirit of the Constitution for strengthening the role of Panchayats in the financing and delivering public services is a correct priority and should remain pivotal issue. Recognising the benefits of decentralisation, it is essentially required to induce Panchayats to mobilise more resources, to stimulate infrastructure expenditures, to improve the financial management and accountability aspects of local government finances, and to provide them with an adequate, dependable and continuous source of revenue.

Graphs

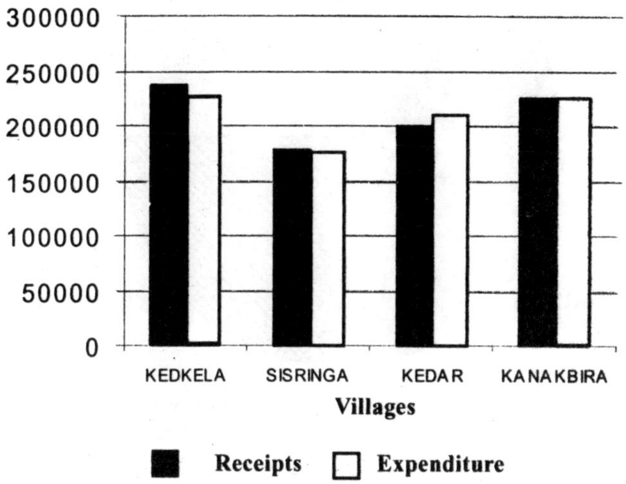

GRAPH 1 : Annual Average of Receipts and Expenditure of Sample Gram Panchayats

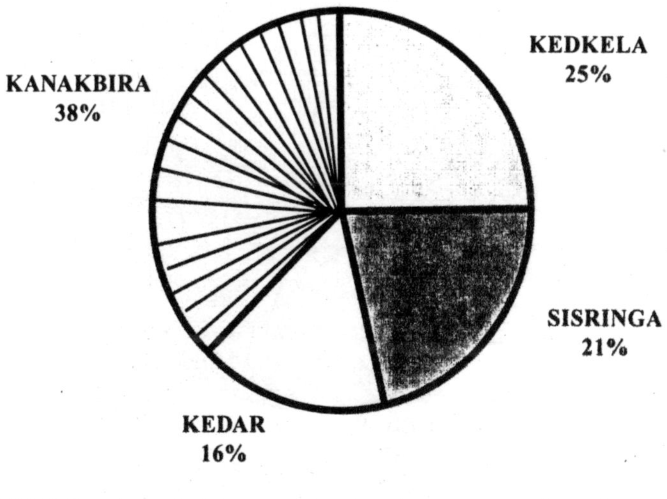

GRAPH 2 : Annual Average of Assigned Revenue to Total Receipts of Sample Gram Panchayats

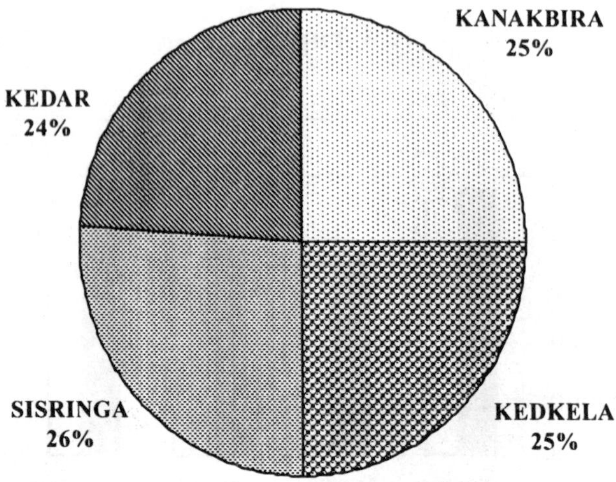

GRAPH 3 : Annual Average of Assigned Revenue and Grants to Receipts of Sample Gram Panchayats

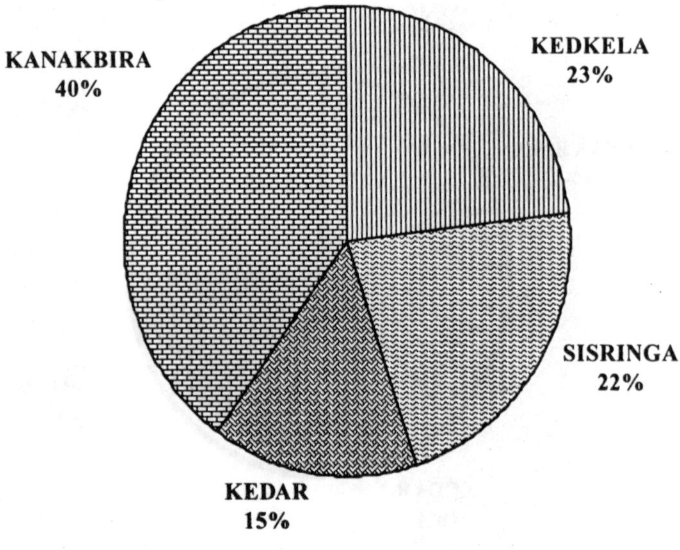

GRAPH 4 : Annual Average Assigned Reverue to Expenditure of Sample Gram Panchayats

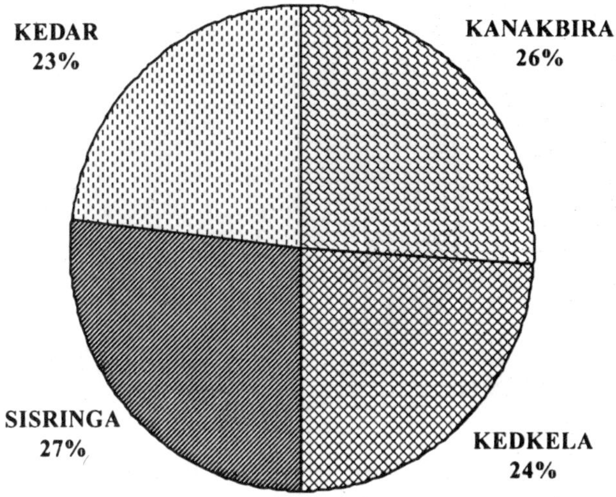

GRAPH 5 : Annual Average of Assigned Revenue and Grants to Expenditure of Sample Gram Panchayats

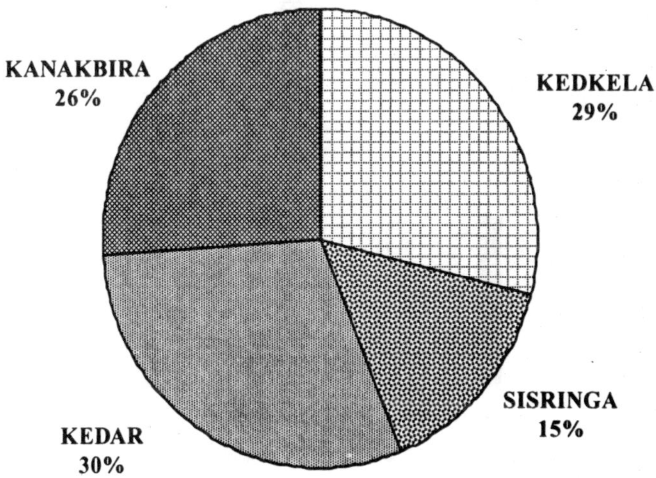

GRAPH 6 : Annual Average of Own Income to Receipts of Sample Gram Panchayats

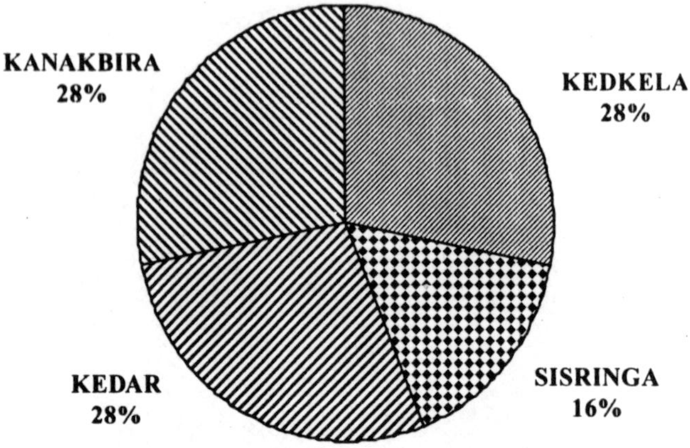

GRAPH 7 : Annual Average of Own Income to Expenditure of Sample Gram Panchayats

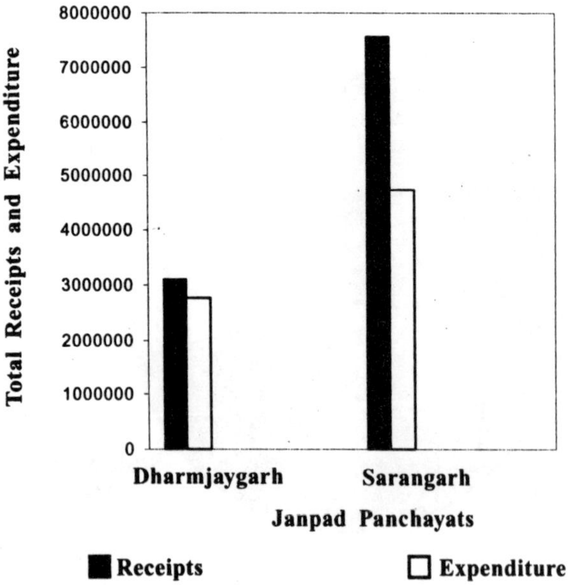

GRAPH 8 : Annual Average of Receipts and Expenditure of Sample Janpad Panchayats

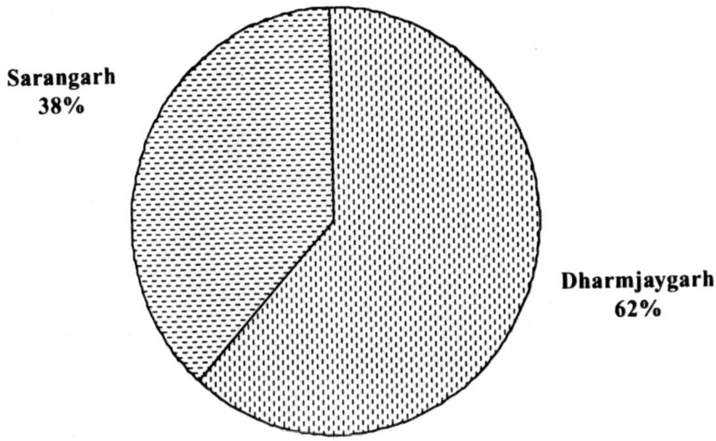

GRAPH 9 : Annual Average of Assigned Revenue to Receipts of Sample Janpad Panchayats

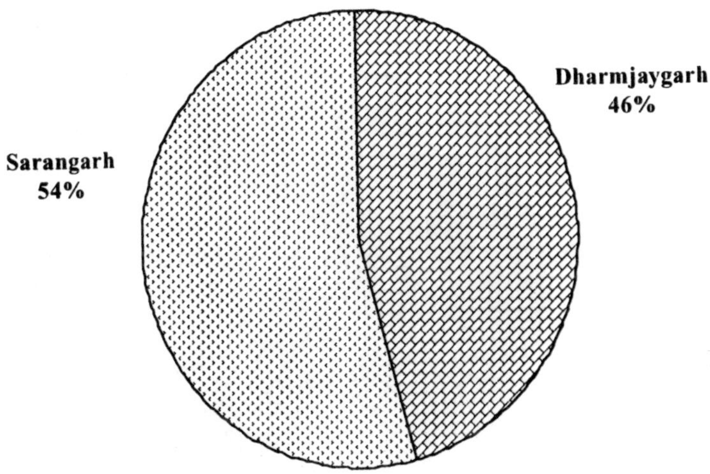

GRAPH 10 : Annual Average of Grants to Receipts of Sample Janpad Panchayats

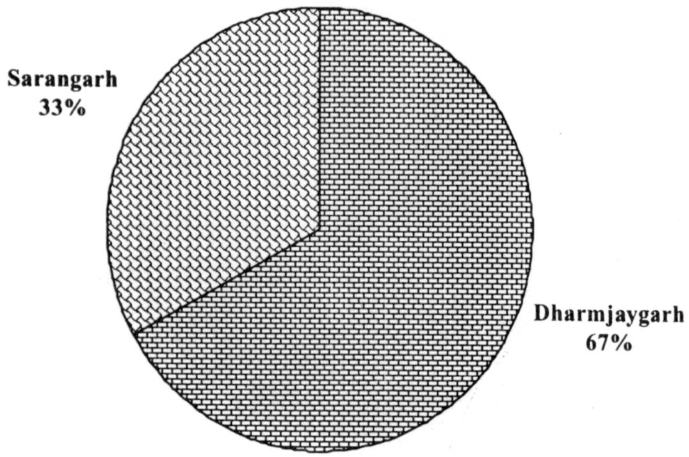

GRAPH 11 : Annual Average of Assigned Revenue to Expenditure of Sample Janpad Panchayats

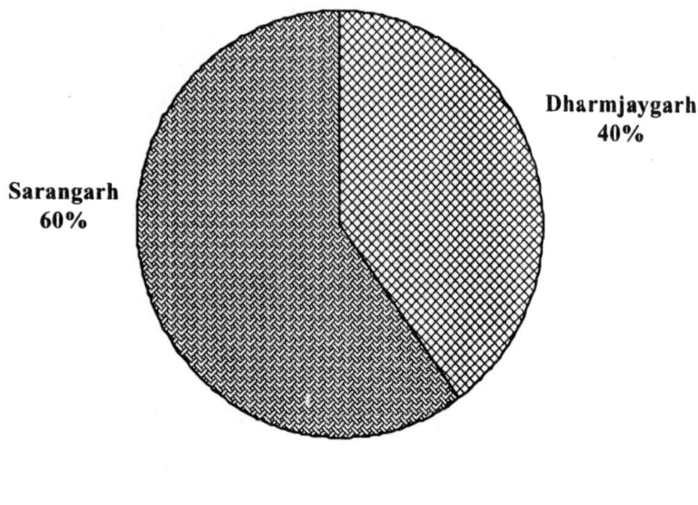

GRAPH 12 : Annual Average of Grants to Expenditure of Sample Janpad Panchayats

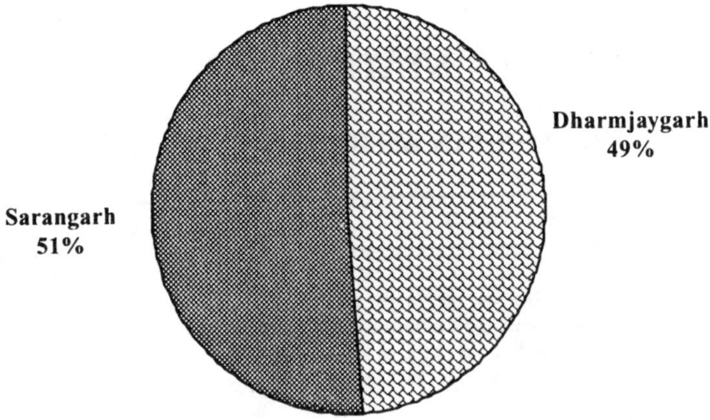

GRAPH 13 : Annual Average of Assigned Revenues and Grants to Receipts of Sample Janpad Panchayats

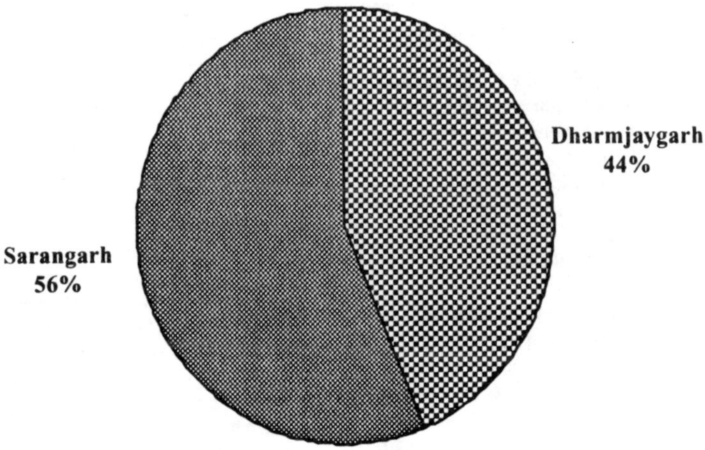

GRAPH 14 : Annual Average of Assigned Revenues and Grants to Expenditure of Sample Janpad Panchayats

STATEMENTS

STATEMENT - 1.1

TAX AND NON-TAX ASSIGNED TO GRAM PANCHAYAT

OBLIGATORY TAXES

1. A property tax on the lands or buildings or both, the capital value of which including the value of the land is more than six thousand rupees other than
   (a) the buildings and lands owned or vested in the Union or State Government, Gram Panchayat, Janpad Panchayat or Zilla Panchayat.
   (b) the buildings and lands or positions thereof used exclusively for religious or educational purpose.
2. A tax on private latrines payable by the occupier or owner of the buildings to which such latrines are attached when cleaned by Gram Panchayat agency.
3. A light tax, if the Gram Panchayat has made light arrangements.
4. A tax on person, exercising any profession or carrying on any trade or calling within the limits of Gram Panchayat area.

NON-TAX SOURCES

1. Market fees on persons exposing goods for sale in any market or at any place or any building or structure therein belonging to or under the control of the Gram Panchayat.
2. Fees on the registration of cattle sold in any market or in any place belonging to or under the control of the Gram Panchayat.

OPTIONAL TAXES, FEES, ETC.

1. A tax on building not covered under item (1) of Schedule I.
2. A tax on animals used for riding, driving, drought or burden or on dogs or pigs payable by the owners thereof.
3. A tax on the bullock-carts, bicycles, rickshaws used for hire within the limits of Gram Panchayat area.
4. Water rate where the Gram Panchayat makes arrangements for regular supply of water.
5. Any other taxes, which the State Legislature has power to impose under the Constitution of India.

NON-TAX SOURCES

1. Fees for the use of sarais, dharmshalas, rest houses, slaughterhouses and encamping grounds.
2. Fees for drainage where the Gram Panchayat has introduced system of drainage.
3. A tax on persons carrying on the profession of purchaser, agent, commission agent, weigh man, or a measure within the meaning of Madhya Pradesh, Krishi Upaj Mandi Adhiniyam, 1972 (No. 24 of 1973). In the area of Gram Panchayat excluding the area of a mandi.
4. A fees payable by the owners of the vehicles other than motor vehicle, where such vehicles other than motor vehicles enter the Gram Panchayat area.
5. A temporary tax for special works of public utility.

OBLIGATORY TAXES	OPTIONAL TAXES, FEES, ETC.
	6. A tax for the construction or maintenance of public latrines and a general scavenging tax for removal and disposal of refuse.
	7. Fees for bullock-cart stand and tonga stand.
	8. Fees for temporary structure or any projection over any public place or temporary occupation thereof.
	9. Fees for grazing cattle over the grazing grounds vested in the Gram Panchayat.

[The powers to impose obligatory and optional taxes by Gram Panchayat under the old MPPA, 1981 and 1990 in Schedule I, of Section 67(1) are same in the new Act of 1993 in Schedule I of Section 77(1). Therefore, there is no change in taxation powers in pre- and post-73rd Amendment.]

STATEMENT - 1.2

RATE OF TAXES OF GRAM PANCHAYAT

RATE OF BUILDING TAX

RATE PREVAILING BEFORE 73RD AMENDMENT [Sub-section (1) of Section 81 of MPPA, 1962 as per rules of April, 1966]			EXISTING RATE [Sub-section (2) of Section 77 of MPPA, 1993 and as per rules of February 29, 1996]		
Particulars	Minimum	Maximum	Particulars	Minimum	Maximum
1. On Building of capital value exceeding Rs. 1,000 but not exceeding Rs. 2,000 2. On building of capital value exceeding Rs.2,000	1. 20 Paise per Rs.100 of the capital value or fraction thereof. 2. Rupee 1 per 500 Rupees of the capital value or fraction thereof but not more than Rs.100.	1. 30 Paise per Rs. 100 of the capital value or fraction thereof. 2. Rupees 1.50 per 500 Rupees of the capital value or fraction thereof but not more than Rs. 150.	1. On building of capital value exceeding Rs. 6,000 but not exceeding Rs. 12,000. 2. On building of capital value exceeding Rs. 12,000.	1. 20 Paise per Rs. 100 of the capital value or fraction thereof. 2. Rupee 1 per 500 Rupees of the capital or fraction thereof but not more than Rs. 100	1. 30 Paise per Rs. 100 of the capital value or fraction thereof. 2. Rupees 1.50 per 500 Rupees of the capital value or fraction thereof but not more than Rs. 150

RATE OF PROFESSION TAX

RATES PREVAILING BEFORE 73RD AMENDMENT [As per rules of April 1966 and under Section 81(1) of 1966 Act.]			EXISTING RATE [As per rules of February 29,1996 and under Section 77(2) of MPPA, 1993]		
Annual Income (Rs.)	Minimum (Rs.)	Maximum (Rs.)	Annual Income (Rs.)	Minimum (Rs.)	Maximum (Rs.)
500 to 1000	1.00	2.00	11000 to 15000	100.00	200.00
1001 to 2000	2.00	4.00	15001 to 20000	150.00	300.00
2001 to 4000	4.00	8.00	20001 to 30000	200.00	400.00
4001 to 6000	8.00	12.00	30001 to 40000	300.00	600.00
6001 to 8000	12.00	16.00	40001 to 50000	450.00	900.00
8001 to 10000	16.00	20.00	—	—	—
More than 10,000	20.00	30.00	More than 50,001	650.00	1400.00

RATE OF VEHICLE TAX

RATE PREVAILING BEFORE 73RD AMENDMENT [As per rules of October 12, 1962 and under Section 82(2) of 1962 Act]		EXISTING RATE [As per rules of February 29, 1996 and under item 3 of Schedule II of MPPA, 1993]	
Particulars	Rate	Particulars	Rate
1. Rate of tax payable by owner of vehicle under Section 82(2)	1. Rs. 2 per vehicle per annum.	1. Rate of tax payable by owner of vehicle under item (3), Schedule-II of the Act.	1. Rs.10 per vehicle per annum.
2. A fee payable by owners of vehicle other than motor vehicle are kept within Gram Sabha area under Section 82 (h)	2. Rs. 1 per vehicle per annum.	2. A fee payable by owners of vehicle other than motor vehicle where such vehicles enter the Gram Panchayat	2. Per vehicle Rs. 5 per day.

RATE OF OPTIONAL TAXES

Rate of fees on persons exposing Goods for sale in any market or place belonging to or under the control of the Gram Panchayat or for the use of any building or structure thereon.

Particulars	Minimum	Maximum
1. For every plot measuring not more than one square metre.	1. 20 Paise per day or Rs. 2 per month.	1. 20 Paise per day or Rs. 4 per month.
2. For every additional space of one square metre or part thereof	2. 5 Paise per day or Rs. 1 per month.	2. 10 Paise per day or Rs. 2 per month.
3. For goods brought to the market for sale	3. 3 Paise per basket or head load (not being a bag) or 10 Paise per bag or 40 Paise per cart load.	3. 5 Paise per basket or head load (not being a bag) or 20 Paise per bag or 75 Paise per cart load.

RATE OF OTHER FEES

RATE PREVAILING BEFORE 73RD AMENDMENT [As per rules of October 12, 1962 and under Section 82(2) of 1962 Act]		EXISTING RATE [As per rules of February 29, 1996 and under item 3 of Schedule II of MPPA, 1993]	
Particulars	Rate	Particulars	Rate
1. Rate of fees for use of sarai, Dharmshalas, etc. under Section 82(G)		1. Rate of fees for use of sarai, Dharmshalas, etc. under item (4) of Schedule II of the Act	
(i) Varandah	Rs. 0.12	(i) Varandah	Rs. 0.50
(ii) Small Room 3×3 metres or less	Rs. 0.25	(ii) Small Room 3×3 metres or less	Rs. 2.00
(iii) Big room (More than 3×3 metres)	Rs. 0.50	(iii) Big room (More than 3×3 metres)	Rs. 4.00
(iv) Rooms furnished with furniture	Rs. 1.00	(iv) Rooms furnished with furniture	Rs. 8.00
(v) Encamping ground upto 3×3 metres	Nil	(v) Encamping ground upto 3×3 metres	Nil
(vi) Encamping ground above 3×3 metres	Rs. 0.06	(vi) Encamping ground above 3×3 Metres	Rs. 0.30
2. Slaughter House	Rs.0.50 per animal	2. Slaughter House	Rs. 2.00 per animal
3. Water rate piped water system per tap	Rs.1.00 per month	3. Water rate piped water system per tap	Rs.20.00 per month
4. Drainage fee value of building above Rs. 10,000	Rs.6.00 per annum	4. Drainage fee	1% of capital value of building per annum
5. Fees for buyer, broker, commission agent	Rs. 4.00 per annum	5. Fees for buyer, broker, commission agent	Rs.25.00 per annum
6. Fee on cart stands/ tonga stand	Rs. 4.00 per vehicle/annum	6. Fee on cart stands per tonga stand	Rs.20.00 per vehicle per annum
7. Fee for grazing cattle on grazing land	Rs. 4.00 per cattle/per annum	7. Fee for grazing cattle on grazing land	Rs.20.00 per cattle per annum

STATEMENT - 1.3

TAX AND NON-TAX ASSIGNED TO JANPAD PANCHAYAT

OBLIGATORY TAXES

1. A Tax on theatre or theatrical performances and other performances of public entertainment.

OPTIONAL TAXES

1. Development tax on agriculture land.
2. Additional Stamp duty.

NON-TAX SOURCES

1. Fees for any licence or permission for use and occupation of lands or other properties vested with it.

[Before 73rd Amendment, obligatory taxes, optional taxes and non-tax revenue sources under sub-section (1) & (2) of Section 67 of MPPA, 1981 and sub-section (1) of Section 75 of MPPA, 1990 is the same after the 73rd Amendment under sub-section (1) of Section 77 of MPPA, 1993 for Janpad Panchayats.]

RATES OF TAXES OF JANPAD PANCHAYATS

1. Entertainment Tax:

	Before 73rd Amendment [Under sub-section (2) of Section 157 of 1962 Act and as per rules of December 11, 1963]		After 73rd Amendment (Under Section (2) of section 77 of MPPA, 1993 and as per rules of February 29, 1996)	
	Minimum (Per show)	Maximum (Per show)	Minimum (Per show)	Maximum (Per show)
1. Cinema	Rs.5	Rs.10	Rs. 10	Rs. 20
2. Drama Circus	Rs.5	Rs.10	Rs. 7	Rs. 15
3. Carnival fete Tamasha, Wrestling Performance	Rs.3	Rs.5	Rs. 5	Rs. 10
4. Any other performance or amusement	Re.0.50	Re.1	Rs. 5	Rs. 5

The rules on entertainment tax lay down the condition that any amusement that is not open to the general public on payment will be exempted. The tax is payable by the manager organising the show. In the event of any breach of any rule the offender shall be punishable with fine which may extend to five hundred rupees.

2. *Fines and Penalties :*

(i) Encroachment fine Rs. 1000.
(ii) Removal from posts if such person does not give charges. Penalty worth Rs. 1000.
(iii) In case the fees on market fair is not paid, fine of Rs. 50 is imposed on the defaulter and if the fine is also not paid, penalty of Rs. 5 per day is imposed till the amount is paid in full.

3. *Ferry:*

Janpad Panchayat auctions it.

OTHER REVENUE SOURCES

Apart from the powers vested under the Act for raising own resources, the PRIs have been delegated powers to mobilize resources by leasing water bodies (Tanks) within their jurisdiction for fisheries development as follows:

Upto 10 hectares	:	Gram Panchayat
Upto 10 to 100 hectares	:	Janpad Panchayat
Upto 100 to 2000 hectares	:	Zilla Panchayat

STATEMENT - 1.4

ELEVENTH SCHEDULE *vs.* DEVOLUTION OF FUNCTIONS TO JANPAD PANCHAYAT

S.No.	Functions	Transferred Fully/Partly	Government Notification regarding transfer to functions
			No.356/MS/Panchayat/94 dated
1.	Agriculture including agricultural extension	YES	8.8.94
2.	Land improvement, implementation of land reforms, land consolidation and soil conservation	NO	
3.	Minor irrigation, water management and watershed development	YES	8.8.94
4.	Animal Husbandry, dairying and poultry	YES	"
5.	Fisheries	YES	"
6.	Social Forestry and Farm Forestry	YES	"
7.	Minor Forest Produce	NO	—
8.	Small Scale Industries, including Food Processing Industries	NO	—
9.	Khadi, Village and Cottage Industries	YES	8.8.94
10.	Rural Housing	YES	"
11.	Drinking Water	YES	"
12.	Fuel and fodder	NO	
13.	Roads, culverts, bridges, ferries, waterways and other means of communication	YES	23.8.94
14.	Rural electrification including distribution of electricity	NO	—
15.	Non-conventional energy sources	YES	—
16.	Poverty alleviation programme	YES	8.8.94
17.	Education including primary and secondary school	YES	"
18.	Technical training and vocational education	NO	1994
19.	Adult and non-formal education	YES	1994
20.	Libraries	YES	1994
21.	Cultural activities	YES	1994
22.	Markets and fares	YES	8.8.94
23.	Health and sanitation including hospitals, primary health centres and dispensaries	YES	8.8.94
24.	Family Welfare	YES	"

S.No.	Functions	Transferred Fully/Partly	Government Notification regarding transfer to functions
25.	Women and Child Development	YES	8.8.94
26.	Social Welfare, including welfare of the handicapped and mentally retarded	YES	"
27.	Welfare of weaker sections and in particular of SC and STs	YES	"
28.	Public Distribution Systems	NO	—
29.	Maintenance of Community assets	YES	1994

STATEMENT - 1.5

ELEVENTH SCHEDULE *Vs.* DEVOLUTION OF FUNCTIONS TO ZILLA PANCHAYAT

S.No.	Functions	Transferred Fully/Partly	Government Notification regarding transfer to functions
			No.356/MS/Panchayat/94 dated 8.8.94
1.	Agriculture including agricultural extension	YES	8.8.94
2.	Land improvement, implementation of land reforms, land consolidation and soil conservation	NO	—
3.	Minor irrigation, water management and watershed development	YES	"
4.	Animal husbandry, dairying and poultry	YES, except dairying and poultry	"
5.	Fisheries	YES	"
6.	Social Forestry and Farm Forestry	YES	"
7.	Minor Forest Produce	NO	—
8.	Small Scale Industries, including Food Processing Industries	NO	—
9.	Khadi, Village and Cottage Industries	YES	8.8.94
10.	Rural Housing	YES	"
11.	Drinking Water	YES	"
12.	Fuel and fodder	NO	—
13.	Roads, culverts, bridges, ferries, waterways and other means of communication	NO	—
14.	Rural electrification including distribution of electricity	NO	—
15.	Non-conventional energy sources	YES	30.10.94
16.	Poverty alleviation programme	YES	8.8.94
17.	Education including primary and secondary school	YES, only secondary school	30.10.96
18.	Technical training and vocational education	NO	—
19.	Adult and non-formal education	YES	1994
20.	Libraries	YES	"
21.	Cultural activities	YES	"
22.	Markets and fares	NO	—
23.	Health and sanitation including hospitals, primary health centres and dispensaries	YES	8.8.94

S. N.	Functions	Transferred Fully/Partly	Government Notification regarding transfer to functions
24.	Family Welfare	YES	6.10.95
25.	Women and Child Development	YES	8.8.94
26.	Social Welfare, including welfare of the handicapped and mentally retarded	YES	"
27.	Welfare of weaker sections and in particular SC and STs	YES, only school education	"
28.	Public Distribution Systems	NO	—
29.	Maintenance of Community assets	NO	—

STATEMENT - 1.6

ELEVENTH SCHEDULE *vs.* DEVOLUTION OF FUNCTIONS OF GRAM PANCHAYAT

S.No.	Functions	Transferred Fully/Partly	Government Notification regarding transfer to functions
			No.356/MS/Panchayat/94 dated 8.8.94
1.	Agriculture including agricultural extension	YES	8.8.94
2.	Land improvement, implementation of land reforms, land consolidation and soil conservation	YES, only land reform	"
3.	Minor irrigation, water management and watershed development	YES	"
4.	Animal Husbandry, dairying and poultry	YES, except dairying and poultry	"
5.	Fisheries	YES	"
6.	Social Forestry and Farm Forestry	YES	"
7.	Minor Forest Produce	NO	—
8.	Small Scale Industries, including Food Processing Industries	NO	—
9.	Khadi, Village and Cottage Industries	YES	8.8.94
10.	Rural Housing	YES	"
11.	Drinking Water	YES	"
12.	Fuel and fodder	NO	—
13.	Roads, culverts, bridges, ferries, waterways and other means of communication	YES	25.1.94
14.	Rural electrification including distribution of electricity	NO	—
15.	Non-conventional energy sources	YES	8.8.94
16.	Poverty alleviation programme	YES	25.1.94
17.	Education including primary and secondary school	YES	8.8.94
18.	Technical training and vocational education	NO	—
19.	Adult and non-formal education	YES	25.1.94
20.	Libraries	YES	30.10.96
21.	Cultural activities	YES	—
22.	Markets and fares	YES	25.1.94

S.No.	Functions	Transferred Fully/Partly	Government Notification regarding transfer to functions
23.	Health and sanitation including hospitals, primary health centres and dispensaries	YES	25.1.94
24.	Family Welfare	YES	"
25.	Women and Child Development	YES	"
26.	Social Welfare, including welfare of the handicapped and mentally retarded	YES Excluding mentally retarded	28.10.096 25.1.94
27.	Welfare of weaker sections and in particular SCs and STs	YES	25.1.94
28.	Public Distribution Systems	YES Only preparation of ration card	"
29.	Maintenance of Community assets	YES	"

STATEMENT - 1.7

HONORARIUM AND OTHER PERKS TO ELECTED REPRESENTATIVES

ZILLA PANCHAYAT

	President	Vice President	Members
1. Honorarium	Rs.1500 per month	Rs.1000 per month	—
2. Entertainment Allowance	Rs.500 per month	Rs.250 per month	—
3. Daily allowance	Rs.40 per diem on tour	Rs.40 per diem to tour	Rs.40 per diem on tour
4. POL charges	212-300 litres depending upon numbers of Janpads	—	—
5. House Rent	Rs.2500 per month	—	—

JANPAD PANCHAYAT

1. Honorarium	Rs.750 per month	Rs.500 per month	—
2. Entertainment allowance	Rs.250 per month	Rs.150 per month	—
3. Daily allowance	Rs.20 per diem on tour	Rs.20 per diem on tour	Rs.20 per diem on tour

GRAM PANCHAYAT

1. Service allowance	Sarpanch Rs.1800 per annum	—	—

Bibliography

Bahl, Roy and B.D. Miller, (1983), *Local Government Finance in the Third World*, Pregger Special Studies, USA.

Bardhan, P. (1996), "Decentralised Development", *Indian Economic Review*, Vol.32.

Bardhan, R. and C. Wallich (1993), Fiscal Decentralisation and Inter-governmental Relations in Transition Economies: Towards a Systematic Framework of Analysis, Policy Research Working Papers, No. 1122, World Bank, Washington, D.C.

Madhya Pradesh Me Navgathit Tristariya Panchayato ko Adhik ke Pratynyojan ke Paripatron ka Sankalon, 1997.

Madhya Pradesh Panchayat Adhiniyam, 1981

Madhya Pradesh Panchayat Adhiniyam, 1990

Madhya Pradesh Panchayat Adhiniyam, 1993

Oates, Wallace, (1972) *Fiscal Federalism*, Harcourt Brace Joranovich, New York.

Oommen, M.A. (1998), *Devolution of Resources to Rural Local Bodies*, Institute of Social Sciences, New Delhi.

Oommen, M.A. and A. Dutta (1995), *Panchayats and Their Finances*, Institute of Social Sciences, Concept Publishing Co., New Delhi.

Pillai, G. K. (1986), *Local Finance in a Developing Economy*, B.R. Publishing Corporation, Delhi.

Report for Rural Local Bodies, Madhya Pradesh State Finance Commission, 1996.

Shah, A. (1991), Perspectives on the Design of Inter-governmental Fiscal Relations, Policy Research and External Affairs working papers No.726, World Bank, Washington, DC.

Singh, S.K. (1999), State Finance Commissions and Devolution of Funds, *The Asian Economic Review*, Vol.41, No.2, Hyderabad.

Singh, S.K. (1999), Punjab Finance Commission Report: A criteria, *Journal of Rural Development*, Vol.18(2), NIRD, Hyderabad.

State Local Fiscal Relations in India, Manohar Publication, 1998.

Sury, M.M. (1998), *Fiscal Federalism in India*; India Tax Institute, New Delhi.

Unpublished Report on "Functional and Financial Devolution on PRIs: A study across the states", Mahila Chetana Manch, Bhopal, September 1999.

Wiseman, J. (1981), *Revenue Sharing between Central and Local Governments in a Developing country with a unitary system of Government*, Institute of Social and Economic Research, University of York.

Index

Absorptive capacity, 5
Accountability, 134
Action Taken Report (ATR), 7, 8, 102, 119, 123
Additional sources, 173
Additional stamp duty, 30, 72-75, 83-85, 92-94, 103-105, 129-32
cess on, 74-77
collection of, 77
Administration, 62-64
Administrative functions, 15
Agency functions, 13
performance of, 5
Agricultural product market, 113
Agricultural production, 76
Allocation formula, 5
Anganwadi, 19
Animal husbandry, 5
services, 15, 19
Annual plan, 117
Assessment, 75-77
Assigned revenues, 11, 28, 69-75, 84-87, 128-32
annual average, 85-86
composition and trends in, 80-81
distribution of shares, 78
performance of, 85
Autonomy, 5

Basic function, 13, 83-84
Beneficiaries, 13, 19-20
Block Development Officer, 23
Block grants, 87
Budget, 103
Building tax, 33

Cash crops, 76
Central Finance Commission, 88, 120
Cess, 70, 74-77, 130-32
rates, 30
Challenging, 3, 120
Chaukidar, 21-22
Civil services, 18
Commercial tax grants, 131
Commission fund, 103
Committed grants, 108
Compulsory taxes, 29-30
Conditional grants, 6, 87
Consolidated fund, 3, 88
Constraints, 9
Contagious diseases, control of, 19
Credibility, 120

Data collection, 8-9, 127
Demonstration, 62
Departmental activities, assignment of, 15-16
Department of School education, 17
Development purpose grants, 89-96
Development tax, 128
Dharamjaygarh, 50
Dichotomy, 68
Discrimination, 22
Discretionary services, 6
District Panchayati Raj fund, 71
Draingage tax, 33
Drinking water resources, 83
DRDA, 22, 23

Economic development, 2, 12
EDP, 58
Education, 17, 95
Elected representatives, honorarium and perks to, 156
Employment schemes, 67
Employment Assurance Scheme, 17
Enforcement power, 58
Entertainment tax, 42, 69, 128
Essential services, expenditure on, 62-63
Establishment grants, 87, 111
Expenditure, 28, 85-86
trends and patterns of, 59
Exploitation, 73

Family benefit scheme, 67
Fairs and festivals, 50

Ferry services, 32
Financial autonomy, 133
Financial conflict, 2
Financial devolution, 68, 129
Financial problems, 57
Fiscal composition, 128
Fiscal decentralisation, 133
Fiscal federalism, 3-5, 68, 126
Fiscal transfers, 69-70, 131-32
Flow of funds, 78
Forest revenue, 113
Functional assimilation, 20
Functional devolution, 23, 28
Functional responsibilities, 13
Funds, allocation of, 62
    devolution of, 12, 94-95
    distribution of, 120-22, 133
        guidelines, 104, 106
    major sources of, 130
    periodicity release, 79-80, 119-20
General purpose grants, 6, 89-94, 96, 107, 122, 131-32
Global sharing, 103, 133
Gram Panchayats, 9, 31-52
    additional cess income, 30
    additional stamp duty, 77-78
    assigned revenues, 80-83, 91-92
    central and state scheme, 19-20
    development and maintenance function, 13-14, 154-55
    expenditure of, 37, 60-64
    functionwise expenditure data, 59-60
    funds distribution, 79-80
    grants devolution to, 94-95
    higher tax collection, 42
    house tax rate, 42
    land revenue cess, 72, 77-78
    levying tax procedure, 31
    non-tax revenue of, 31-52, 46-47, 49-50
    organisational structure, 24
    powers and responsibilities, 18
    receipts of, 34-35
    staff strength of, 27
    tax and non-tax revenue collection, 57-58, 142-43
    tax revenue income, 38-40
    taxes, rates of, 144
Gram Sabhas, 8, 56
Grants, categories, 87-88
    types of, 6-7, 68-69, 89-90, 131
    utilization, 64-65
Grants in aid, 86-88
Gross-revenue, 120-21

Hand pump maintenance, 17
Honorarium, 20, 93-94, 156-57
House tax rate, 42

Incentive grants, 7, 108
Income, sources of, 30
Indira Awas Yojana, 17
Infrastructural development work, 99
Integrated child development programme, 16
Integrated Rural Development, 17
Inter-district distribution, 105
Inter-governmental fiscal transfers, 3, 5-6
Inter-jurisdictional spillovers, 4-5
Inter-se distribution of funds, 78-89
Internal resource mobilisation, 33
Itemised sharing, 6

Janpad Panchayat,
    additional cess income, 30
    additional stamp duty, assigned to, 72-73, 77-78, 82
    administrative functions, 15
    assigned revenues, 78-79
        devolution of, 90-92
    chief executive officers, 21-22
    development programmes, 9, 15-16
    devolution of function to, 150-51
    educational department, 19
    expenditure data, 45-46, 63-65
    funds distribution of, 79-80
    internal sources, 56-57
    grants allocation, 56, 89-90
        devolution of, 93
    land revenues cess, 72
        distribution, 77
    levying tax procedure, 31
    management function, 15
    non-tax revenue sources, 31-32, 50
    optional taxes of, 30
    organic agriculture, promotion of, 19
    organisational structure, 25
    per capita assigned revenue, 82-83
    per capita income and expenditure, 49-50

programme implementation, 16
receipts of, 43-44
resources composition, 47-48
staff structure, 20-22, 27
tax and non-tax assigned to, 50, 148-49
tax revenues, 42-43
taxation power, 29-30
Jawahar Rojgar Yojana, 17

Land revenue, 69, 70-71, 74-75, 103, 129-30, 130-32
assessment of, 75-76
cess of, 72-74, 75-78
criteria for distribution, 77-79
mode of collection, 77
Land revenue code, 75
Levying tax, procedure for, 31, 74-75
Loans, 69, 100-101
Local bodies, grants-in-aid to, 3, 7-8
Local revenue mobilisation, 33, 37-38
Lump sum non-recurring grants, 112

Madhya Pradesh Mineral rules, arrangement of, 73-74
Madhya Pradesh Panchayat Land Revenue Cess and Stump Duty Fund, 70-71
Madhy Pradesh Panchayat Act, 12
Madhya Pradesh Panchayati Raj Adhiniyam, 13, 28, 127
Madhya Pradesh Panchayati Raj Fund, 71
Management Functions, 15
Mandi tax, 58, 128
Master Plan, 76
Matching grants, 7
Minor irrigation, 95
grants, 87, 95
Minor minerals, 81
exploitation of, 73-74, 129-30
royalty of, 75-79
MLA Local Area Development Fund, 99-100
Mobilizing tax revenue, 42

National Finance Commission, 3
New dispensation, 50, 82, 127
Nidhi, 72
Non-tax revenue, 102, i28
sources of, 31-32, 129

Obligatory functions, 15, 18, 103, 120
local services, 6
non-tax sources, 31-32
taxex, 29, 50
Observation method, 8
Old age pension, 67
Oommen, M.A., 5, 7, 88
Operationalisation, 128
Optional taxes, 29-30

Panchayats,
expenditure classification, 59
financial composition, 28
devolution on, 68-59
sources of, 28
status, 7, 12
flow of funds, 69-70
functional devolution on, 12-26
Panchayat Karmi, 20-21, 57, 93, 131
Panchayati Raj Institutions (PRIs), 8-10
assigned grants, distribution of, 8, 70
funds release to, 79-80
land revenue distribution, 77
Paripatron ka Sankalan, 15
Patwari, 16, 77
Per capita assigned revenue, 83
Performance budget, 117
Perfunctory function, 13
Pisciculture, 19
Poppy cultivation, 76
Poverty alleviation programme, 20
Predictability, 5
Primary school building maintenance, 19
Professional tax, 29, 33, 38, 41, 69
Property tax, 29, 31, 33, 36
Public expenditure, 68-69
Public Health Engineering Department, 17
Public well, maintenance of, 18

Raigarh district, 9
Rational fiscal relations, 126
Rational grants system, 88
Ratlam district, 76
Regional disparities, 121
Registration of cattle, 49
Resources mobilisation, 2
Revenue collection, 56
districtwise distribution, 116
sources of, 58-59

Road maintenance grants, 88
Royalty, 73-84
Rural development funds, 2, 114

Sanitation tax, 36
Sarangarh, 50
Sarpanch, 19
Sensitisation programme, 57
Sharing revenues, 69, 121
Shiksha Karmi, 63, 67
Social Justice, 12
Social Security Pension Yojana, 17
Specific area component plan, 112, 114
Specific purpose grants, 6, 89-94, 96, 108, 112
Spillovers, 4-5
Sponsored programmes, 124
Stamp duties, 69-70, 83-85, 92-94, 129-32
Staffing pattern, 22-23
State Finance Commission (SFC), 1, 3-7, 36, 49, 56, 72, 88, 91, 95, 100, 120
- grants, 58-59
- recommendations, 3-7, 74, 78, 81, 88-89, 92, 102, 104-119, 131-32

State Panchayat Fiscal Relations, 1-2, 7-8, 68-69
Sury, M.M, 5
73rd Constitutional Amendment, 1-2, 29, 36, 49, 123, 126

Tax administration, 31, 58
Tax collection, 128-29
- mechamism of, 36

Tax revenues, 28-29, 33-34, 49-50
Tax sharing, 6
Taxes, periodic assessement, 58
- defalter of payment, 32
- determination, 3
- rates of, 29-30

Tax and non-tax revenues, 28
Taxation powers, 29-31
Tenth Finance Commission, 89, 121
- funds, 132
- grants, 58, 98, 100, 131

Three-tier panchayat, 2, 18
- programmes, 13

Transparency, 5
Tribal area sub-plan, 114

Unconditional grants, 87-88
Uneconomic policies, 5

Veterinary dispensaries, 19
Village assistance, 20-21
Village development fund, 113
Village Panchayat, 8-9
Village and Khadi Industry Board, 16

Water supply system, 38-95
Water resource department, 16
Wiseman, J., 6

Zilla Panchayat, 9
- additional stamp duty distribution, 77-78
- additional cess income, 30
- assigned revenue, devolution of, 75-76, 80-83, 152-53
- centrally sponsored scheme, 17
- construction irrigation plants, 16
- departmental activities, 15-18
- development grants, 132
- expenditure of, 65-66
- functions devolution, 15, 18-20
- funds distribution, 79-80
- general purpose grants, 131-32
- grants devolution, 89-90, 92
- internal sources, 51
- land revenue cess, 72, 77-78
- levying tax procedure, 31
- non-tax revenues, 31-32, 46, 51-52
- new dipensation, 51
- new restructuring pattern, 22
- organisational structure, 26
- per capita expenditure, 53-55, 67-68
- staff pattern, 20-23, 27
- taxation powers, 30-31